LNWR LIVERIES

Frontispiece
'The LNWR at its Zenith. Norton Bridge, 1913.'
From an original painting by Gerald Broom GRA

LNWR LIVERIES

| Edward Talbot | George Dow | Philip Millard | Peter Davis |

Published by the

HISTORICAL MODEL RAILWAY SOCIETY

GEOFFREY PLATT

Geoffrey Platt, to whom this book is dedicated, died on 25th July 1980. For nearly twenty years he was Sub-Dean of the Faculty of Engineering at King's College, London University.

He joined the Historical Model Railway Society soon after its foundation in 1950 and became devoted to its interests. He served continuously on its Executive Committee, with a break of only two years, from 1955 until his retirement in 1975, occupying successively the posts of Secretary, Deputy Chairman in 1963 and Chairman in 1972. In 1976, after moving from Purley to Holywell, he set up the new North West and North Wales Area of the Society, centred upon Chester.

In addition, he was the Society's Company Steward for the London & North Western Railway, upon which he was a recognised authority. By the time of his death, he had completed considerable research in preparation for the publication of this book, the bulk of the material in which is derived from his work. It is for this reason that it is dedicated to him.

Geoffrey Platt modelled in 7mm scale and was an excellent draughtsman. Those who knew him will remember him for his extensive railway knowledge, his modesty and his warm personality.

President HMRS

THE HMRS

About the publishers of this book

The Historical Model Railway Society is a charitable educational Trust, celebrating its 35th Anniversary in 1985. The Society has certain clearly defined objectives and its primary concern has been to foster the research and recording of information relating to the railways of the British Isles, and to ensure that this information is disseminated widely, and in particular for the benefit of model makers to help them build accurate and authentic models. The Society has over 1700 members world wide and they comprise not only active researchers and model makers but also those simply with a broad affection for Britain's railway heritage.

The Society has an active publications policy and this is a key way of ensuring that the fruits of members' research are passed on to a wide audience. The Society has made a particular study of liveries, recognising that this aspect, though of considerable importance to model makers, has often been poorly recorded. Earlier livery registers have dealt with the Caledonian, London & South Western, Southern, Midland and Great Western Railways. The Society also publishes a high quality quarterly Journal and a regular Newsletter both of which are distributed free to members. The Society's activities encompass all periods of railway history, and whilst at first it was primarily concerned with the recording of the pre-grouping scene today both the grouped companies and British Railways have strong followings within its membership.

The Society has extensive collections of drawings and photographs, which are particularly strong in their coverage of carriages and wagons, as well as an extensive library. Information is also circulated through a system of Company Stewards, each specialising in a particular company and acting as a clearing house for the exchange of information, so that members with a particular interest in one company have a definite point of contact for information and inquiries. There are also local area groups meeting regularly in different parts of the country.

Further information and a membership prospectus is available from: P.A.Ray, Hon.Membership Secretary, 7 Field Style Road, SOUTHWOLD, Suffolk, IP18 6LA.

CHARLES RENNIE MACKINTOSH 1868–1928

About the design of this book

Charles Rennie Mackintosh achieved consummate skills as an architect, furniture designer, graphic designer, textile designer and artist in watercolours. Today, with the wisdom of retrospect, he is judged one of the great figures of the European movement known as Art Nouveau and he enjoys a cult following in the world of art and design. Yet, in his working lifetime, too many of his contemporaries indulged in character assassination, and the uncomprehending establishment, fearing change, eventually forced him into family exile.

In his journeyings between Glasgow, London and Europe, Mackintosh became a customer of the Caledonian Railway and, further south, of the London & North Western Railway. He may well have taken dinner in the elegant saloon depicted at the opening of Chapter 6. He was commissioned by W. J. Bassett-Lowke to re-build a house for him at 78 Derngate, Northampton, and to design the furniture, fittings and decor. How many models, including those of the LNWR, went to pay for such a luxury, one wonders.

Passionately believing in the artist-craftsman with all-round skills, Mackintosh designed his own unique alphabet and numerals. In his designs he favoured the square and elongated oblong as geometrical shapes. His most creative work was contemporary with the great period of the London & North Western Railway, and so his alphabet has been chosen for the decorative headings of this book and his geometric motifs echoed in its design.

Peter A. Esgate

ISBN 0 902835 08 4

Designed by Peter A. Esgate

Printed in England by J.B.Shears & Sons Ltd, Basingstoke, Hants.

CONTENTS

DEDICATION   THE HMRS

PREFACE & ACKNOWLEDGEMENTS

INTRODUCTION

ARMORIAL DEVICES	1
PERMANENT WAY & WORKS	8
SIGNALS & SIGNAL BOXES	20
BUILDINGS, STRUCTURES & STATION EQUIPMENT	26
LOCOMOTIVES	42
COACHING STOCK	86
GOODS ROLLING STOCK	128
ROAD VEHICLES	146
NORTH LONDON RAILWAY	158
EPILOGUE	172
BIBLIOGRAPHY	178
INDEX	179

PREFACE & ACKNOWLEDGEMENTS

Much of the information in this book is based on work by Geoffrey Platt, whose researches were cut short by his death. Overall responsibility for the project was then assumed by Philip A.Millard, the locomotive section being written by Edward Talbot. As the book came nearer to publication, the latter assumed the role of general editor and further major contributions were made by George Dow and Peter Davis.

It is now impossible to identify many of those who originally supplied information to Geoffrey Platt and so to acknowledge their contributions. Certainly prominent among them was J.P.Richards, whose immense fund of knowledge on the LNWR is equalled by his kindness in making it available to others. His help has been invaluable to the present authors also. Other notable contributions were made by A.M.Gunn, Harry Jack and Laurie Ward.

The present authors have greatly appreciated the wholehearted encouragement of Mrs Kathleen Platt, who has allowed generous access to Geoffrey's material and shown considerable forebearance in the face of every delay. Major contributions to the locomotive section were made by W.A.Camwell and Jack Hassall, while Alan Gettings supplied many drawings, especially of name and numberplates, and Bob Hunt made the drawings of lining details. Alison Millard has always offered much encouragement and toleration to Philip during his work on the book. R.M.Casserley made an invaluable contribution to the carriage section, as did several of the staff at Wolverton Works, especially Cyril Webb, whose patient indulgence is particularly appreciated. Geoff Williams spared no effort to provide material for the section on buildings and structures, while D.J.Clarke, Richard D.Foster, Tony Lyster, D.N.Ratcliffe, G.N.Webb and Mike Williams also gave generous help in various ways. Andrew Dow willingly provided photographs and took several especially for the book, and Arthur Hancox and Michael Cox provided almost all the information and material for the North London Railway chapter. Gerald Broom painted two pictures specially as illustrations. John Edgington, Technical Information Officer at the National Railway Museum, York, has been a constant source of help, and The Keeper has kindly granted permission to publish Crown Copyright pictures from the NRM collection. The staff at the Public Records Office, Kew, have been unfailingly courteous. To all these people, and to any who have been inadvertently overlooked due to the somewhat chequered career of the book's preparation, we extend our grateful thanks.

Finally, but by no means least, thanks are also due, from the HMRS as well as ourselves, to Peter Esgate for designing the book, negotiating with the printers and generally taking charge of the whole production process.

Edward Talbot ▪ **George Dow** ▪ **Philip A.Millard** ▪ **Peter Davis**

INTRODUCTION

Several years ago the Historical Model Railway Society embarked on the publication of a series of detailed studies of the liveries of various railway companies for the benefit particularly of modellers and of railway enthusiasts in general, and this book is the latest in that series. Its purpose is to place on record as much information as can now be assembled about the liveries of the greatest of the British pre-grouping companies, the London & North Western Railway.

Fortunately, despite its size and its lengthy existence, some seventy-five years, this is a relatively easy task. The company vigorously pursued policies of standardisation virtually from its inception, and certainly from the late 1850s, so that detail variations are few. Furthermore, although it participated in several joint railways (at least as many as the Midland), they were operated with the other owning companies as truly joint railways. Each company used its own trains over the joint line, and departmental responsibilities, such as for signalling, were shared between them. Thus no pseudo-independent companies, such as the Midland took part in, have to be accounted for. Similarly, with one exception, the LNWR had no satellite companies operating their own trains, as did the GWR in the 19th century and the Midland in the early 20th, nor, after its early expansion, did it absorb numerous smaller companies, as did the GWR. The one satellite exception, the North London Railway, was closely associated with the parent company and after 1908 was absorbed by it.

Nevertheless, because of the passage of time, much information, particularly about the Victorian period, cannot now be established or verified, and even for the later period there are several areas of doubt. At this stage, however, it seems unlikely that many of these problems can ever be satisfactorily resolved and so there is little to be gained by delaying publication any further.

I

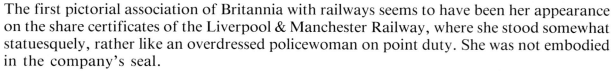

ARMORIAL DEVICES

by **George Dow**

The first pictorial association of Britannia with railways seems to have been her appearance on the share certificates of the Liverpool & Manchester Railway, where she stood somewhat statuesquely, rather like an overdressed policewoman on point duty. She was not embodied in the company's seal.

On the 1846 seal of the LNWR, however, Britannia was the centrepiece. Seated with her trident and looking towards the right, she was flanked by the British lion and her Union Jack-bedecked shield. And in the background a train puffed its way across a multi-arched viaduct. This placid scene was reflected in many LNWR staff uniform buttons and on some types of the company's stationery.

A simplified version consisting only of Britannia, trident, lion and shield, became the standard emblem of the LNWR. But its splendid simplicity was somewhat spoiled by the mass of predominantly gilt Victorian decor with which it was surrounded when transfers were made of it.

There were four designs. The first of them, wherein Britannia looks leftwards, was displayed mainly on locomotives. It was photographed in 1875 on carriages of the LNWR train which participated in the Newark brake trials and is also to be seen on a 6-wheeled carriage photographed in 1881. It measures $13\frac{3}{8}''$ wide $\times 12\frac{1}{2}''$ high and became the standard emblem for certain classes of locomotive on which it first appeared in June 1878.

At about the same time a different transfer, $9\frac{1}{2}''$ wide $\times 9\frac{1}{2}''$ high, was produced solely for the carriage stock. The central part of it was more akin to the scene on the seal. It was followed by another design, for road vehicles such as omnibuses, which was similar to the locomotive emblem, save for differences of detail in the ornamentation. It measures $8\frac{3}{8}''$ wide $\times 6\frac{1}{4}''$ high.

The final armorial transfer was for steamships. It was an altogether neater design because all the surrounding decor has disappeared. It is $16\frac{1}{2}''$ in diameter. Britannia still faces left, but the lion has assumed a rather Metro-Goldwyn-Mayer look!

Irish outpost of the LNWR was the Dundalk, Newry & Greenore Railway, on which were followed the traditions of Crewe and Wolverton in the design and colours of locomotives and rolling stock. But it had its own coat of arms, which embellished the carriages.

The earliest transfer of it depicts Britannia, now devoid of shield and lion, clasping hands with Hibernia, who holds a harp and is accompanied by a shaggy grey Irish greyhound. In the left background there is a train consisting of a $2-2-2$ locomotive with a 6-wheeled tender and 4-wheeled carriage, in the centre a paddle steamer and on the right the pier and lighthouse at Greenore.

It is not known when the second transfer replaced the first. Basically it was of the same design, but there were differences in detail. The greyhound is sleeker and blue-black in

colour, as if to emulate LNWR locomotives, and the train in the background is formed of a 4–4–0 with 4-wheeled tender and a bogie coach. Both DNGR designs measure $15\frac{1}{8}''$ wide × $12\frac{3}{4}''$ high.

Britannia also appeared, alongside the Lancashire & Yorkshire armorial device, in the transfers made for the parcels vans of the Preston & Wyre Railway. This was a joint undertaking of the two companies which served the area lying between Preston, Lytham, Blackpool and Fleetwood. There were two versions, the only difference being that the titles of the owning railways were reversed. These transfers were printed in two sizes, $10''$ wide × $6\frac{1}{2}''$ high and $6''$ wide × $4\frac{3}{4}''$ high.

Seven years after its incorporation in 1846, the East & West India Docks & Birmingham Junction Railway changed its name to the more appropriate North London Railway. The original title is reflected in the $8\frac{1}{2}''$ wide × $10\frac{3}{4}''$ high transfer of the armorial device which adorned the teak-finished passenger carriages of the line. A similar design was to be seen on the company's 25mm-diameter brass buttons on staff uniforms. The anchor in the top left quarter, its shank emblazoned with a lion rampant, indicates the maritime connection of the railway; Birmingham and London are denoted in the top right and bottom left quarters respectively; and in the fourth quarter is illustrated the entrance gateway to the West India Import Dock, which was opened in 1802.

Plate *1*
Staff uniform button, 25mm in diameter, from the David Swan collection.

Andrew Dow

2

Plate *2*   *Andrew Dow*
Coat of arms transfer displayed usually on locomotives.

Plate *3*   *Andrew Dow*
Coat of arms transfer displayed usually on passenger carriages.

Plate 4   *Andrew Dow*
Coat of arms displayed on road vehicles.

Plate 5   *Andrew Dow*
Armorial transfer used on steamships.

Plate 6
First design of armorial transfer used on the DNGR.

Plate 7

Second design of armorial transfer used on the DNGR, and monogram.

Plate *8*
Transfer used on parcels vans jointly owned by the LNWR and LYR.

Andrew Dow

Plate *9*
Coat of arms transfer of the North London Railway.

Andrew Dow

Plate 10 *(C.P.Davis collection)*
'The Finest Permanent Way in the World' seen at Elmhurst Crossing in 1898 or 1899. Standard 90lb rail in 30'0" lengths resleepered with eleven sleepers per panel instead of the original ten. The ballast is broken blast furnace slag laid on a bottom pitching of large stones. The immaculate condition of the permanent way is matched by that of the cess and grass verge.

2

PERMANENT WAY & WORKS

by **Peter Davis**

Constituent and Absorbed Companies

The Liverpool & Manchester Railway was laid with fish-bellied wrought iron rails 15′ long weighing 35lb per yard in chairs spaced at 5′ intervals and fastened to stone blocks set diagonally. On embankments and over peaty ground transverse oak sleepers were used. One remarkable feature was that the inner edge of the rail was shaped to match the tyre profile. As laid, the inner rails of double track were only four feet apart but this was gradually increased to six feet whenever relaying was undertaken.

The London & Birmingham, Manchester & Birmingham and Crewe & Chester Railways were also laid with this type of Stephensonian track although by that time the fish-bellied rail originally used on the LMR had given way to a double headed rail weighing 60lb per yard.

The Wigan Branch Railway, engineered by Charles Vignoles, was laid with 45lb per yard 'T' section rails 15′ long but to a very primitive standard. Relaying with double headed rails was accomplished within a short time.

The Grand Junction Railway used Locke's double headed rails of 84lb per yard in chairs with wooden keys on kyanised (after 1840, creosoted) timber sleepers. The last were intended as a stopgap and to be replaced by stone blocks as a more 'permanent' way. However, even by 1845, according to the *Railway Share-Holders Manual*, 20 miles of track still lay on sleepers and 62 miles on stone blocks while $\frac{1}{2}$ mile was carried on longitudinal sleepers over viaducts.

The North Union Railway used mainly Vignoles rail on cross sleepers while the Lancaster & Preston used 65lb double headed rails on timber sleepers for embankments and stone blocks in cuttings. The Chester & Holyhead as opened to Bangor in 1848 had 75lb double headed rails in chairs, weighing 20-24lb with fir keys, laid on triangular or rectangular section sleepers of 9′0″ length. The Saltney-Chester section was equipped with fish-plates under licence from the Permanent Way Company in August 1855 but the whole of the C & H was relaid with 80lb rails in 1858-9 in preparation for the improved services introduced after the company became part of the LNWR.

Post Amalgamation Developments

Until 1853 rails were supplied to the LNWR from contractors but their deteriorating quality led to the establishment of a rail mill at Crewe. From July of that year 21′0″ long iron bullhead rails and fish-plates — which superseded joint chairs — were produced there until 1876. The first Bessemer steel rails were laid in Crewe station in November 1861 and shortly afterwards taken up for show at the London Exhibition of 1862. More steel rails were laid at Chalk Farm in 1862 but the use of steel was limited, because of expense,

8

to special locations where high wear and tear was experienced. An interesting experiment in reducing maintenance costs took place in 1866 when two miles of iron rails on the Shrewsbury and Birmingham section were continuously welded using a semi-portable forge developed at Crewe. The world's first continuously welded rail was produced by the LNWR!

In 1864 Webb developed a steel-headed rail, the foot and web being of wrought iron, and this economical compromise was increasingly used in place of purely iron rails until in 1875 a new rolling mill was commissioned in conjunction with the Steelworks to produce the cheaper Siemens-Marten steel rails in 30′0″ lengths. From 1876 only steel rails were produced, of 84lb per yard for main line use and 75lb for branches.

The next development came in 1887 when 90lb per yard was adopted as standard for main-line use and 80lb for secondary routes. Furthermore, according to Findlay in *The Working and Management of an English Railway*, 10 miles of line laid with 60′0″ long rails were in use by 1889 in awkward locations like tunnels and viaducts. One assumes that these rails were welded because the Crewe rail mill was not modified to produce rails of that length until 1893. From April 1894 60′0″ rails were used in relaying main lines; the first length to be so treated was at Betley Road south of Crewe.

Standard Permanent Way

The standard 30′0″ track panel as laid before 1894 had ten sleepers of 9′0″ × 10″ × 5″; this was increased to eleven on sharp curves. The later 60′0″ track panel included 22 sleepers of 9′0″ × 10″ × 5″ and one 9′0″ × 12″ × 5″ sleeper at each end. When lengths of permanent way laid with 30′0″ rails were re-sleepered in later years 11 or 12 sleepers were used depending upon the weight of traffic to be carried.

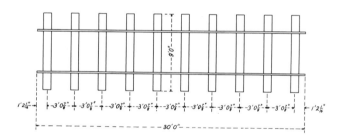

Figure 1 *(C.P.Davis)*
Standard track panel with 30′0″ rails.

30′0″ rails were fished with pairs of plates which curved under the rail. The outer plates had grooves rolled in them to stop the square-headed bolts from turning. Hexagonal nuts were used until about 1890 when square ones were adopted. The new type of fishplate which accompanied the 60′0″ rail was easier and cheaper to roll, one pattern sufficing for use both inside and outside the rail. The bolts now had a projection next to the head to suit elongated holes punched in the plate, and their heads were domed instead of square. The final development in rails came in 1905 when a bullhead section weighing 95lb per yard was adopted for main line use. This later became the British Standard. At the same time 85lb bullhead rails became standard for secondary lines.

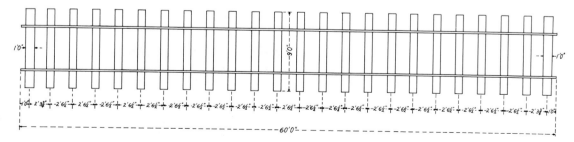

Figure 2 *(C.P.Davis)*
Standard track panel with 60′0″ rails.

Keys were of compressed English oak, 6″ long, fitted to the outside of the rail and shaped to fill the rail web completely. After insertion they swelled to fill the gaps between ridges cast in the curved outside jaw of the chair. As early as 1864 steel keys were being produced at Crewe but the use of these remained very limited in LNWR days.

Sleepers were of Baltic fir (Pinus Sylvestris) laid 'heartside' down. They were machine bored and adzed to a standard depth on the sap side at Willesden works, and a number of other locations, and afterwards creosoted. About 32lb of creosote went into each sleeper. There was a hair felt pad of about $\frac{1}{4}''$ thickness between sleeper and chair. From about 1881 there were always small numbers of iron and steel sleepers in experimental use at a number of locations. The standard length for sleepers was 9'0" as on other British standard gauge railways until a timber shortage after the First World War necessitated a change to 8'6".

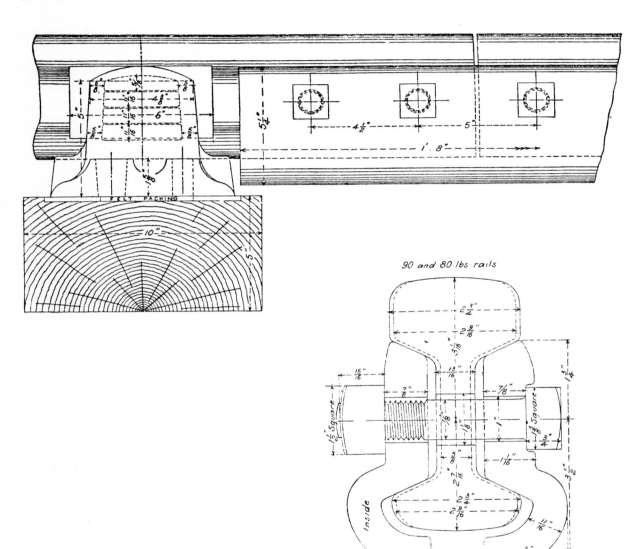

Figure 3a *(Railway Engineer)* 30'0" rail, fishplates and fishbolt.

Chairs measuring $14\frac{3}{8}'' \times 7\frac{3}{4}''$ and weighing 45lb were used in plain track. At the end of each 60'0" panel, and on points and crossings a slightly larger chair $14\frac{3}{8}'' \times 9\frac{3}{4}''$ was used.

With regard to fastenings, the LNWR was unique among the pre-group companies in using iron, later steel, screws as favoured in Continental practice. In addition to two of these, each chair carried two iron spikes. The screws were $6\frac{1}{2}''$ long, the shank tapered in diameter from $\frac{7}{8}''$ to $\frac{13}{16}''$ and were at first made of galvanised iron, with hexagonal heads. After about 1905 steel screws with square heads became standard. A tight fit in the chair was obtained by the use of oak ferrules. The iron spikes $6'' \times \frac{13}{16}''$ were arranged diagonally opposite the screws.

10

Figure 3b *(C.P.Davis)*
Fishplate and bolt for 60'0"
rail.

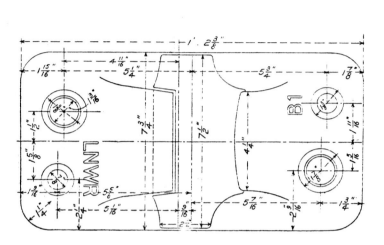

Figure 3c *(Railway Engineer)*
45lb chair.

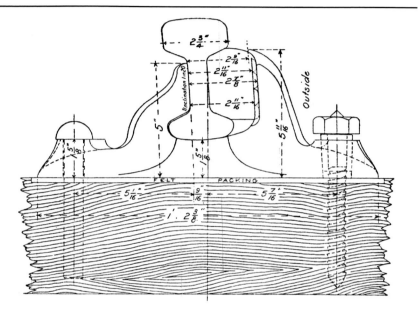

Figure 3d *(Railway Engineer)*
Fastenings. The galvanised iron
screw had a hexagonal head, the
pointed 'pip' was added by
Webb and was intended to ensure that plate-layers used the
correct spanner instead of a key
hammer to drive it home.
However, when walking the line
on his own, a ganger would
prefer to leave the 1¾" chair
spanner in the hut and take a
nut to place over the 'pip' so
that he could still use the key
hammer. The square-headed
steel screw was introduced in
1905.

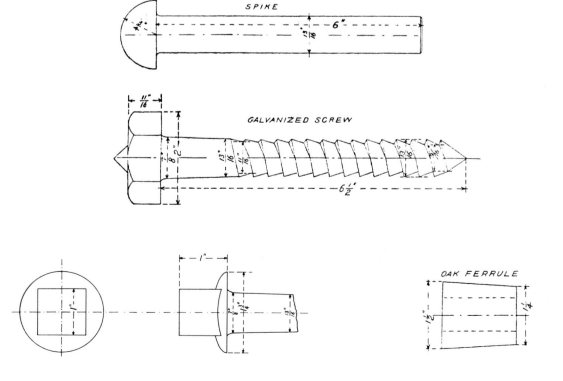

SPIKE

GALVANIZED SCREW

OAK FERRULE

Plate 11 *(G.M.Perkins)*
A watering point on the Central Wales line near Knighton in or around 1910. The tank and pipe would be painted dark grey and the woodwork tarred. The remote location is rather reminiscent of North American practice, but the permanent way is typical of the LNWR. The 30′0″ rails have again been resleepered with eleven to the length. Note the 'Webb' hexagonal headed chair screws with oak ferrules and the distinctive arrangement of stone ballast, bottom pitching and cess.

Compared with that of the other large main line railways of Britain, the permanent way of the LNWR was, until the early 20th century, rather on the light side when one considers the weight and volume of traffic carried. This in turn had a considerable influence upon locomotive design; until the advent of the 60′0″ panel the maximum permitted axle load was 15t 10c. However, a combination of careful formation and excellent ballast, together with the highest standards of routine inspection and maintenance enabled the company to claim, with some justification, that it owned the 'finest permanent way in the world'. The ballast was probably the largest single contributory factor in this claim. For many years the main routes were ballasted with broken blast furnace slag, screened to 2″, except in the north and in Wales where hard stone was available locally. Iron slag was considered the ideal material; sufficiently toxic to prevent the growth of weeds, it did not crumble to dust and therefore maintained excellent drainage. After the turn of the century it became increasingly difficult to obtain adequate supplies, however, and broken granite was substituted.

Plate 12 *(G.Williams)*
Chairs in use on secondary lines and sidings often had only three fastenings instead of the four found on main lines.

Plate 13 *(G. Williams)*
Later type of joint chair for 60'0" rail with only the two screw fastenings, and dated 1915.

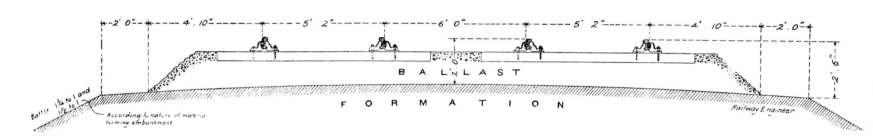

Figure 4 *(Railway Engineer)*
Cross section of double track. The top ballast, whether stone or slag, was passed through 2" diameter rings.

Lineside Equipment

The railway's boundaries were marked by cast iron posts which were painted white while the letters, raised $\frac{1}{8}$", were painted black. Gradient posts were made of wood with $1\frac{1}{4}$" thick cast iron letters and figures screwed on and painted black. The posts and arms were painted white although the lower 1'3" or so of the post was often black or dark brown. Mile and quarter mile posts were also of wood with cast iron figures, being finished in a similar style to gradient indicators but with a plain white post. Both gradient and distance indication was normally placed on the 'Down' side of the line. In the late LNWR period and into LMS days concrete was used in replacing these indicators but the designs remained the same.

Lineside fencing varied from place to place. A five-bar design of creosoted fence was most commonly found. Typically, the posts stood 5'0" above ground level and 8'0" apart, there being some local variations. A rather more expensive fence was used especially on roads leading to bridges and level crossings or for station approaches. The posts were of oak and the top rail, fastened with iron straps, of pine. These fences were usually painted white but could also appear in station colours (see Chapter Four).

Two types of iron fence were also quite widespread. A horizontal railed type, for preventing access to the railway by animals, was made in 7'0" lengths while the 'unclimbable' fence, denying easy access by humans, came in 6'0" lengths. Both types appeared in either black or red oxide.

Bridges and viaducts were identified at either end by an oval plate attached to the left hand side facing oncoming trains. Measuring 1'6" × 1'0" with 4" figures, the plates had black characters and edging on a white ground. Buildings were also identified by number; this being displayed either on a cast plate or as separate screwed on cast figures.

Plate 14 *(G. Williams)*
A hand operated switch at Llanberis. The lever is 2'0" long and the weight 11" in diameter. The hexagonal chair screws are set at 2'5" centres, this being the normal spacing for switch and crossing timbers.

Plate 15 *(D.N.Ratcliff)*
Wooden stop blocks. The frames were of 1'3"×1'3" timbers while the buffing plank was 1'6"×10".

Plate 16 *(G.Williams)*
Rail-built stop blocks in a siding at Aylesbury. An intermediate buttress was added to each frame on running lines.

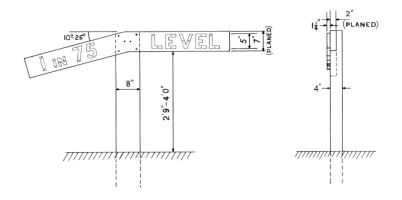

Figure 5a *(C.P.Davis)*
Wooden gradient boards.

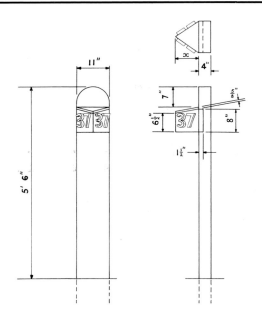

Figure 5b
Wooden milepost. The dimension shown as 'x' varied between approximately 7″ and 10″ according to the number and width of digits to be displayed.

Plate 17 *(G. Williams)*
Cast iron boundary post. There were two distinct patterns; one had a tapered back support with gentle parabolic curve at the top (see J.K.Nelson, *LNWR Portrayed*, p.182) and the other was provided with a parallel back support with a radius at the top. The letter face was identical in both patterns.

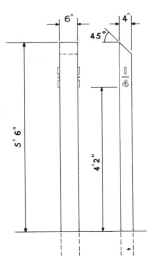

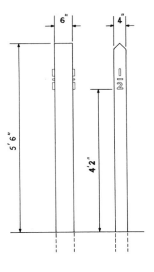

Figure 5c
Wooden quarter mileposts. The left hand elevations depict the post as viewed from the permanent way.

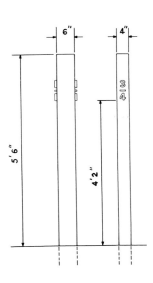

16

Plate 18a/b/c *(G.Williams)*
Wooden mileposts and gradient indicators.

17

Plate 19a/b *(G. Williams)*
Cast iron bridge numberplates. The usual painting style was black characters and edging on a white ground like the less common rectangular plate, which came from the Manchester area.

Plate 20 *(G. Williams)*
Cast iron property numberplate from the signalman's cottage at Aylesbury.

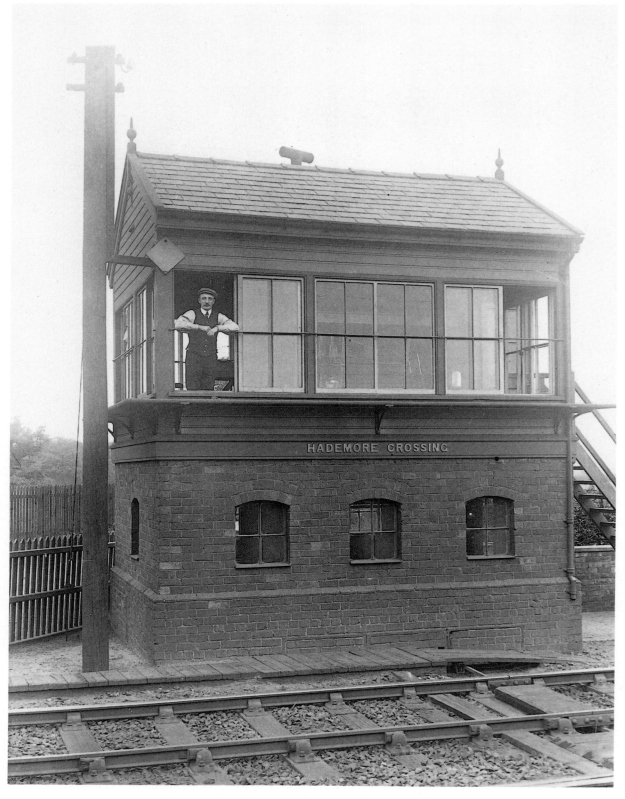

Plate 21   *(E. Talbot collection)*
Hademore Crossing Signal Box was of the standard flat gable type introduced in 1876 and erected here in 1899. The brown and buff colours can be seen together with white window frames. Usually the windows in the locking room also had white frames but here they are either very dirty or painted brown. The white diamond above the signalman denotes that the signalling equipment is in working order. When reversed it showed red, indicating a fault; passing enginemen were expected to observe it and report the fact at their next stopping place so that a lineman could be summoned. There should also be an oval board, normally showing white but with a black reverse side, which applied to the telegraph equipment in the same way. These boards gradually fell into disuse and were officially abandoned in 1911. The name of the cabin appeared in screw-on cast iron letters painted white. In later years the name was surrounded by an oval panel painted red.

3

SIGNALS & SIGNAL BOXES

by Peter Davis

Signals

The red used for signal arms was made with two parts red lead to one part vermilion, the front faces of both distant and home signal arms were finished in this colour; the familiar vertical white stripe became standard in the early 1870s. The backs of the arms were white, with a black stripe after 1873. Wooden arms were painted but the later corrugated steel arms were enamelled.

Signal posts were normally painted with white lead except when experiments with other materials were conducted as when zinc silicate was used as pigment for a short period during 1884 or when special finishes were applied; for example signal posts in the vicinity of Shugborough Park were painted green at the request of the Earl of Lichfield. The foot of the post and all metalwork except the finial was painted red oxide. Guy posts were finished the same as signal posts.

Wrought iron brackets, on gantry and bracket signals, were painted a buff or stone colour in the normal way but from 1887 onwards new brackets were galvanised instead of being painted. However as the protective coating broke down and rusting started these brackets were also painted. Sometimes black was a local substitute for red oxide on signal ironwork but this was always an unofficial practice. Besides appearing in red oxide or black, in later years brackets were sometimes painted white to match the posts. The ironwork of gantries seems usually to have been painted buff or red oxide like brackets, but in the present century was often painted black or grey.

Signals applying to slow and goods lines were fitted with rings of 30″ outside diameter and 3″ wide. From 1883 onwards these were painted black except on the NLR where they were white on the front and black on the rear.

The standard ground disc signal introduced in 1881 had a rotating lamp. When in the 'on' position it displayed a large red painted face bolted onto the body of the lamp around the red spectacle. In the 'off' position a green spectacle was displayed. The back of the lamp body surrounding the small white spectacle was usually painted white to assist the signalman in seeing the position of the signal. The rest of the signal was painted brown. From 1915 miniature semaphore ground signals were introduced. The arms were painted as for full size semaphores but with the raised rim picked out in white. The body and other ironwork were painted brown.

Calling on signal arms were red with vertical white stripe. In the 'on' position the lamp was masked, a small white light being revealed in the 'off' position. Just before the First World War a new pattern of shunt signal was introduced again painted red with vertical stripe but showing a red light in the 'on' position as well as the white light when 'off'. From 1920 this signal was also applied to the calling on function.

Signal Spectacles-An Historical Note

Before 1873 all signal equipment was supplied to the LNWR company by contractors and semaphore signals, operating in slotted posts, displayed the three aspects required under the time interval method of operation. The spectacles were usually mounted separately and showed red, to denote danger, green, for caution, and white for all clear. These colours are used to this day on the railways of Britain when handsignalling at night. A bi-directional signal could be found at wayside stations. The left hand arm- looking in the down direction- was connected to a spectacle on the front of the post having the red glass above the green and covering the lamp mounted on the right hand side of the post. The right hand arm was connected to a spectacle on the back of the post which, because it

Plate 22 *(G.N. Webb)*
Bi-directional station signal supplied by Saxby and Farmer and photographed at Bedford (St Johns) station in the late 1870s. Note the arrangement of spectacles and the ball and spike finial.

was served by the same lamp as the other arm, had the glasses reversed- green above red. Signals of this type can be seen in the background in a number of photographs of small stations even into the present century.

In 1874 the Company began to manufacture its own signalling equipment at Crewe. The first design of semaphore retained the slotted post and ball and spike finial of the Saxby and Farmer signals but often used only one spectacle, therefore at night only two colours were displayed, red and white. It became common practice to lower these arms only as far as the 45° position at which the all clear light was revealed. From 1876 the ball and spike finial gave way to the familiar cast iron cap which remained standard into LMS days. In 1883 a new design of signal with corrugated steel arm and a double spectacle plate operating on a plain post was introduced. The bottom glass was left out of the spectacle to show a white light whenever necessary. The top spectacle contained either a red or a green glass depending upon the function of the signal, stop or distant. From April 1873, to alleviate the difficulty that drivers were experiencing in sighting the correct signals, the danger light in subsidiary signals was altered from red to purple.

Plate 23 *(G.H.Platt collection)*
Standard Crewe slotted post signal of the 1876-1883 period. The back blinder can be seen; in the 'on' position a colour would be seen by the signalman, the white back light showing when the arm stood in the 'off' position.

22

As the number of white lights visible at night increased dramatically during the 'eighties it was becoming very awkward in built up areas for drivers to pick out their own all clear lights. The RCH meeting of 27th July 1893 therefore recommended that the white light in fixed signals be dispensed with leaving only red and green for main signals. Green thus became all clear and at the same time the small green back lights were altered to white. From then on a white light visible from a fixed post, where a red or green should be seen, was to be treated as a danger signal.

Plate 24   *(D.N.Ratcliff)*
Audible Signal, or Shunting Gong, operated by the signalman and used to control movements in station yards. The standard RCH code for audible signalling was usually adopted but there seem to have been a number of local codes in use at specific locations. The painting style was that of other fixed signals.

The purple danger light in subsidiary signals was abandoned in the early 1900s but again the problem of too many red signals presented itself in some locations and was solved by giving some ground signals a white danger light. After 1914 red was adopted as the danger aspect for ground signals controlling exits from sidings or loops to main lines but white lights remained in use in a number of locations until LMS days. It should be remembered too that calling-on signals displayed a white all clear aspect.

Red remained as the caution light in distant signals well into LMS days, yellow was adopted in 1929. All things considered, a great deal of local knowledge was required of pre-group enginemen.

Signal Boxes

The standard colours were those used on station and other buildings; stone (buff), mid-brown (chocolate) and white. Window frames of both upper and lower storeys were white; doors, staircases, floor level fascia board and all ironwork, including cast iron window sills in the lower storey, were brown. In later years barge boards, finials, window surrounds, catwalk and brackets and sometimes corner posts were also painted brown. Otherwise all other woodwork was buff. Local variations, in which parts were brown and which were buff, were common. Since the buff darkened with weathering and the brown tended to fade, it is often difficult to tell one from the other in old photographs. The shade of brown paint used varied from time to time as witnessed by sample boards which inspectors were ordered to prepare for comparison. The buff also varied; the recipe was given in 1885 as:-

> 7lb White lead
> $\frac{1}{2}$lb Yellow ochre
> $\frac{1}{2}$oz Turkey umber

but the 1898 specification called for a somewhat darker shade:-

> 7lb White lead
> 2lb Yellow ochre
> $1\frac{1}{2}$oz Turkey umber

However, certain photographs of stations, taken in the early part of the 20th century, seem to suggest the use of two shades of buff in addition to the brown; in view of this it is possible that the above specifications apply to two distinct shades which were in use at the same time.

Gantry structures were treated the same as those for signals, mostly brown, later grey or black. The name of the box was shown on the fascia board in cast letters painted white and surrounded, at least from the 1900s, with a panel in vermilion red which, officially at any rate, should have had semicircular ends.

For a few years after 1890 some new cabins were treated at Crewe before assembly with 'carbinoleum', a preservative distilled from coal tar. The exact colour of these boxes is not known but would presumably have been somewhat reminiscent of creosote. The finish did not weather well so that the outsides of carbinoleum boxes were retreated or revarnished at intervals of about half the normal three years for painted boxes. Paint would not take on the carbinoleum so that, when it was decided to end the experiment at the turn of the century, these boxes were varnished before being painted in the standard colours.

The interiors of signal boxes were painted stone colour (buff); block shelf, lockers, desk and ironwork were vermilion as applied to signal arms. When the carbinoleum boxes were new they were officially intended to have the external ironwork and stage painted vermilion in addition to the internal fittings.

Plate 25

(HMRS V1673)

Thrapston Station looking towards Northampton in about 1920. Dark buff and light brown seem to be the main building colours here with either light buff or white for the platform fences. White window frames can be seen but the signal posts are all rather dirty, the one in the foreground, being concrete, appears to be unpainted. Two types of platform lamp are in evidence, those with long glass bowls, often referred to as 'bell-jar' lamps, are painted brown and mounted on cast iron posts in brown and buff. The one on the left has had its burner and hood removed. Diamond framed lamps hang from either end of the up platform awning. The awnings are buff with brown brackets, gutters and fascia boards. A standard station seat painted brown with the name in raised letters can be seen below the 'running-in' nameboard which has white cast letters on a black background and a buff surround. The water columns are painted dark grey; the overflow from them is directed through gratings on the platform edge along blue brick courses between the sleepers into brick troughs, with a cast iron grating at one end, placed in the middle of the six-foot. The train is loaded with pig-iron destined for use as ship's ballast.

25

4

BUILDINGS, STRUCTURES & STATION EQUIPMENT

by **Peter Davis**

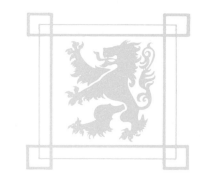

Station Buildings

Wooden station buildings were painted in the same style as signal boxes — buff and brown — sometimes referred to as light and dark buff. These buildings were usually of a standard modular construction. The one in the view of Gowerton is structurally typical but is finished in an unusually dark chocolate brown together with a rather light buff. The usual finish for these buildings includes a lighter brown as well as white on the window frames.

Many wayside stations were provided with wooden huts, assembled from standard components but varying in length according to location and the purpose for which they were built. The most common variant — see the view of Holly Bush — was a lamp room with door at one end and a window at the other. The same basic design also served for staff mess rooms, ground frame and weighbridge huts, goods offices and countless other applications including passenger station offices. For example the lamp room was extended to form a combined small goods warehouse and office, in a separate end room; this variant is extant on the remains of the LNWR Carmarthen branch. A slightly wider version could also be found, an example which survives at Shap is a small goods shed without the separate room, end door or windows. Larger wooden goods sheds were painted in the same style as these small 'Webb' huts.

Stone and brick built station offices were painted in the same colours. Window frames were normally white, surrounds, sills, doors and ironwork were brown and other woodwork such as bargeboards was buff. Where outside walls were rendered they were also painted buff while casement windows without separate wooden surrounds were often brown, especially where the adjacent stonework was buff. The station building at Ridgmont is typical of those on the Oxford to Cambridge line. Buff appears to be almost the only colour on the building though doubtless the doors were brown like the posts supporting the lean-to awnings and platform lamps. Oxford LNWR station was a non standard wooden building; here the main colours are light and dark buff — perhaps the window frames are white — while the uprights and cast iron pillars supporting the canopy appear to be light and dark brown below 'waist' level.

An interesting variation is to be seen in a view of Marsh Gibbon and Poundon taken in or around 1900. All the parts that one expects to see in brown, with the exception of the lower front of the signal box, appear to be a very light shade. Perhaps this is primer and the brown is in the process of application. It was standard practice to instruct painting contractors to apply undercoats of colours which contrasted with the top coat so that a cursory inspection would reveal any skimping of the final coat. Later views of this station by the same photographer (Newton) taken in 1904 and 1908 show the usual style for a wooden station, the foundation rail, corners, window frames and surrounds and doors being painted brown.

The walls of wooden buildings were painted buff down to ground level until at least the 1900's when it became common to treat the planking up to 'waist' or window sill level with the brown colour.

Plate 26 *(Lens of Sutton)* Gowerton Station looking North just prior to the First World War. The building on the right is constructed from standard modules and finished in a chocolate brown and light buff. The standard footbridge appears to be buff although at smaller stations these were usually grey. The oil lamps on the station building and under the bridge are of an unusual pattern and the 'running-in board' has a white surround.

Plate 27   *(Lens of Sutton)*
Holly Bush on the Sirhowy Valley line looking towards Tredegar in later LNWR days. This view illustrates many standard LNWR items. The small lamp room on the left hand platform with window at one end and door at the other is entirely typical. Just below the ridge the building date is displayed in cast figures and the property number, also in screw-on figures, is on the top rail of the door. The water tank is grey and the footbridge either two-tone grey or brown and buff. On the wall of the *al fresco* gentlemen's convenience on the extreme right can be seen a row of fire buckets suspended on iron brackets from a stout wooden board. Board and brackets are painted vermilion red while the buckets — shown inset — were also red but with black rim and base and white lettering and interior. The letters L&NWR were stamped vertically on the outside just below the rim. The platform fences at this station are the only non standard feature; the paling is continuous and arranged in alternate high and low saw-tooth pairs and, furthermore, is tarred instead of being painted.

27

Plate 28 *(G. Williams)*
Station buildings at Verney Junction assembled from standard 'Webb' hut components. The width is 8'0" and the height to the eaves 7'0".

Plate 29
(R. S. Carpenter collection)
Ridgmont, between Bletchley and Cambridge photographed in August 1917, is typical of the stone buildings on the Oxford to Cambridge line. Note the standard platform trolley in brown with the name and fleet number in white italic characters on the curb rail and a pair of sack trucks with the fleet number on the left-hand shaft.

Plate 30
(Oxford County Libraries)
Oxford London & North Western Railway Station, 1914. The large poster board in the foreground, with its panoramic view of the North Wales Coast, is black with white letters. Two types of fence are visible as well as an interesting assortment of horse drawn carriages.

Plate 31
(Newton collection Leicester Libraries)
Marsh Gibbon and Poundon around 1900. The non-standard station building houses the signal box with bay window. The hut, fence, seat and nameboard are all typical. Ash ballast could be found on some secondary lines of the LNWR into the present century, although by 1904 this particular length had been re-ballasted with better material and the point rodding arranged in a more accessible fashion.

Canopies, Awnings and Footbridges

Smaller canopies like the one at Shap had brown painted cast iron columns, guttering and downpipes. Large platform canopies were usually finished with brown columns and buff brackets, woodwork and awnings. Sometimes the barge boards and gutter fascia boards were painted brown to match the guttering. Awnings might be treated like the one at Glasson, photographed around 1900, with alternate brown and buff, or perhaps light and dark buff, matchboard 'teeth'. At about the same time as this variant was current it became the practice to paint canopy columns buff above waist level.

Station screens were — and still are — a prominent feature of many an LNWR station. There were probably as many painting styles as there were styles of screen, but a general rule seems to be that wooden parts were buff (sometimes the glazing bars were white), while ironwork — columns, girders, guttering and so forth — was brown.

Wooden-clad footbridges were treated in brown and buff in the same manner as buildings and platform fences while iron or steel footbridges serving large passenger stations were also brown and buff. Iron footbridges in remote locations and at small stations were painted in the mid-grey used by the Engineer's Dept. for structural ironwork. In locations within the CME's Dept., leading to steam sheds or workshops, they were usually dark grey or sometimes black.

Plate 32 *(C.P.Davis collection)*
Shap at the turn of the century. The platforms were staggered and at this date had yet to be raised to standard height and are still joined by a boarded crossing with a step between it and each platform. A footbridge was erected when the platforms were raised. The small awning appears all in brown and the fence is high enough to support the small oil lamp without the need for a separate post.

Plate 33 *(C.P.Davis collection)*
Glasson *circa* 1900. The open locking frame with its wooden platform and brown painted ballustrade was a common sight at small stations.

Plate 34 *(G.Williams)*
Details of iron footbridge at Aylesbury.

Station Signs and Ancillary Equipment

Station signs had white edges and white cast letters screwed onto a black or dark blue backing. 'Running in' boards (station name boards) were treated in this style too but the upright posts, and caps, supporting them were usually painted brown or sometimes buff depending on location, that is, whether free standing or incorporated in platform fencing, and before about 1900 the edges were painted buff. There are photographs which seem to suggest however that after about 1900 the edges and reverse sides of name boards were, in some cases, painted in light buff to match the fencing while the posts and caps were dark buff to match the wooden lamp posts.

Lineside notices were finished in the same style as station signs whether of wood with screwed on cast letters mounted on a wooden post or of cast iron mounted on a post made from an old rail. Poster boards displaying timetables, traffic advertising and other poster advertising of the company were painted black with white mouldings and sides and white cut-out letters in the heading space. Where the width of the board was insufficient to allow the title to be given in full, the abbreviation 'L&NWR' was usually employed.

Platform fencing came in a variety of styles. The distinctive design with a combination of vertical planking and horizontal rails was to be found almost anywhere on the LNWR system. The planking was painted buff while the posts and rails were finished in brown as shown in the Ridgmont view. Wooden platforms were usually equipped with a lighter three rail fence which might be either buff or brown according to the local preference. A four railed variant of this can be seen at Marsh Gibbon and Poundon. A paling fence was also very common in two designs. The type of fence seen at Shap for example has three horizontal rails and was usually buff but occasionally brown. The slightly lower version with only two horizontal rails can be seen at Thrapston for example. The size and spacing of uprights and rails as well as the overall height and spacing of pales might vary according to local requirements but a common feature of all these fences, other than the style of painting, was the paling which was of a standard 3″ × 1″ (nominal) section.

The well known LNWR station seat was painted brown with the station name in cast letters upon a recessed panel in the back rail. The name was usually rendered in the same style as other station signs, that is, white letters on black ground, but sometimes, as in the view of Marsh Gibbon and Poundon, this was reversed; however, see remarks above on the subject of undercoat.

Platform trolleys came in several types. The most ubiquitous were sack trucks which were painted brown with the station name and date in white italic script on the outside of the right hand shaft. The number appeared on the left hand shaft as can be seen on the trucks in the Ridgmont view. This view also shows the style of painting applied to the standard four wheeled trolley whereupon the name and number appeared on the curb rail. A third type of barrow resembled a cross between a large sack truck and a hand cart. It had two large wheels and a steel blade, like sack trucks, at one end and two tall wooden legs at the other so that the bed remained horizontal when the trolley was at rest. Trolleys for rugs and pillows were in use at Euston and other large stations in the days before steam heating was generally available on trains. Although the one in the photograph is showing signs of rough handling it can be seen that it is finished in the standard carriage livery of carmine lake and white with a thin ochre line around the edge of the mouldings. The ironwork and lettering were black. The refreshment trolley, in brown livery, was also photographed at Euston and is typical of many in use all over the system.

The earliest and simplest form of station lighting was provided by oil lamps. Although by 1962, when the photograph was taken, the lamp shown here had somehow found its way to Cuddington on the CLC, it is typical of those found on many LNWR stations. The front was 1′6″ high and 1′0″ wide and the depth of the side was 10″. An iron strap was attached to the back to suit the lamp bracket which would be attached to a wall or to a wooden post. The lamp and bracket were brown while the post was all buff, or sometimes brown, at first; the bottom section up to about a foot above ground level was

L & N.W. Station, Rugby. Southern Platform

Plate 35 *(LNWR Society)*
Up platform at Rugby. Note large gas lamps, station clock, train indicator and a variety of signs and notice boards.

Plate 36 *(G. Williams)*
Cast iron lineside notices. Occasionally the lettering appeared in black on a white ground.

brown during the last 20 years or so of the LNWR. A slightly smaller lamp with flat top instead of backward sloping, was in use at small stations in Central and South Wales, and elsewhere, and can be seen in several of the illustrations accompanying this chapter. Like the larger one, it was provided with a concave reflector. Countless stations where there was no town or railway gas supply, and whose traffic was insufficient to justify conversion to electricity, continued to be lit in this fashion until their demise in the Beeching era. Being stored in the lamp room during daylight hours, the lamps were probably used only in the winter months at stations where no early or late trains were provided.

Gas lamps, on cast iron or wooden posts, were installed at stations and in yards in urban areas and painted brown at first. After the turn of the century the posts were often painted buff above the plinth and below the support brackets.

From the turn of the century many of the larger installations were electrically lit. The arc lamp most commonly used had a reinforced glass globe about 1′3″ in diameter. The larger stations had them suspended from the roof but they were also to be found in some outdoor locations like carriage and sorting sidings where they were fed by overhead cables and mounted on wooden posts — for reasons of insulation no doubt — which, with their ladders and platforms, resembled small signal posts and were painted in buff or white with brown plinth and ironwork.

Plate 37 *(G. Williams, E. Talbot)*
Wooden lineside notices.

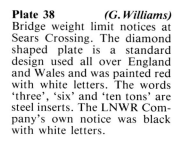

Plate 38   *(G. Williams)*
Bridge weight limit notices at Sears Crossing. The diamond shaped plate is a standard design used all over England and Wales and was painted red with white letters. The words 'three', 'six' and 'ten tons' are steel inserts. The LNWR Company's own notice was black with white letters.

Plate 39a/b   *(G. Williams)*
Warning notices. The cast iron post is cruciform with a circular flange at the top attached by four bolts to a corresponding flange on the base of the cast iron plate. The letters are raised $\frac{1}{4}''$ as is the surround. The blank reverse side also has this raised surround. The plate measures $1'8\frac{1}{2}'' \times 1'0\frac{1}{2}''$. Note the differing styles of lettering. The *in situ* view at Verney Junction shows an 'unclimbable' fence in the background.

Plate 40 *(G. Williams)*
Ornamental style paling fence at Parsley Hay.

Plate 41 *(G. Williams)*
Wooden gate in occupation crossing near Llangunllo. The dates burnt into gate and posts suggest that they were installed in June 1903 (shown as 6/03) but the right hand post has been replaced by one dated 6/11. The wasted state of the middle rails doubtless indicates a sizeable pedestrian traffic over this particular crossing.

Plate 42 *(C.P.Davis collection)*
Standard design of LNWR station seat. Many original examples survive on British Rail but replicas are available commercially.

Plate 44 *(C.P.Davis collection)*
Rug and Pillow Trolley at Euston 1907. The black lettering reads: *Rug or Pillow on hire 6d.* There were still many carriages without steam heating on the LNWR in 1907 but one feels that this was probably one of the last of a once numerous fleet of such vehicles.

Plate 45 *(C.P.Davis collection)*
Refreshment trolley also at Euston 1907. Painted brown with polished brass handrails it is typical of those found at large stations.

Plate 43 *(C. P.Davis collection)*
LNWR sack trucks. Painted brown, the date, in this case 25.7.1906, and the station name appeared in white italic script on the right hand shaft. The fleet number was painted on the left hand shaft.

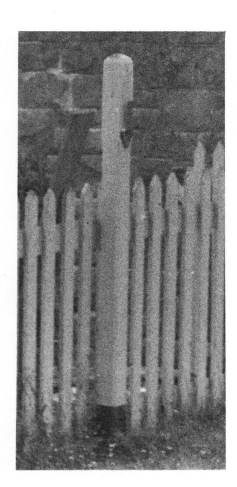

Plate 46a/b *(C.P.Davis collection)*
Removable station oil lamp. (a) One of three distinct designs, this type appears to be the largest. (b) Post for oil lamp, painted buff with brown bracket and bottom.

Plate 47 *(G.Williams)*
Oil lamp permanently mounted on wooden post at Claydon.

Plate 48a/b *(G. Williams)*
(a) Typical gas lamp on cast iron column at Aylesbury.
(b) Standard cast iron lamp post mounted on platform fence at Aylesbury.

Plate 49 *(E. Talbot)*
Large gas lamp as found in goods yards. The gas pipes can be seen on the side of the wooden post which is finished in brown and buff.

37

Other Buildings

The external woodwork of carriage sheds was finished in brown or buff. The ironwork was brown or, especially in smoke polluted locations, dark grey. The interiors were finished with ironwork brown to a height of about 6′0″ and buff above that. Brick or stone walls were limewashed on the inside above the height of 4′0″-6′0″ from rail level and painted dark brown below that.

Loco sheds, or steam sheds as they were called, also had their inside walls painted dark brown up to 4′0″-6′0″ and limewashed above that but it is not possible to state with any authority just how they were painted when new. Surviving photographic evidence seems to suggest standard brown and buff like carriage sheds and engineering works buildings. In later years dark grey seems to have been applied to wood and ironwork both inside and out. Water tanks, water columns and loco yard lamps are believed to have been painted red oxide before the turn of the century and dark grey thereafter. Lamp standards outside loco sheds were originally painted brown but were often white-washed in later years. The glazing bars in the shed lights were also often painted white.

Plate 50 *(C.P.Davis collection)*
Interior of Carlisle carriage shed in about 1905. The rails were laid on longitudinal sleepers.

Plate 51a/b/c *(A.G.Ellis)*
(R.P.F.Rickard 20604)
(a) Interior of loco shed when new, probably Crewe South in 1896. All woodwork, and the walls, are buff but the ironwork is in either very dark brown or oil black. (b) and (c) Cast iron notices displayed at engine sheds.

Plate 52 *(G.H.Platt collection)*
Whitewashed yard lamp and roof glazing bars at Coleham shed Shrewsbury in 1907.

39

Level Crossings

Level crossing gates were painted in the same colours as signal posts, i.e. white with red oxide ironwork. Here, as with signals, local preferences for black or grey ironwork would manifest themselves — albeit unofficially.

Loading Gauges

These were also painted in the signal post colours of white woodwork and red oxide, black or grey ironwork.

Plate 53 *(G. Williams)*
A loading gauge of the type introduced after the First World War seen at Cheddington. The remains of a leather flap can be seen hanging from the right hand side of the gauge bar. When new the leather flaps were triangular and continued the gauge curve down a further 9″ or so on either side. The previous style of all-iron gauge bar was in the form of a continuous curve; the leather modification was introduced to protect the heads of men looking out from modern wide vehicles.

'Changing engines at Stafford in the early 1860s' from an original painting by Gerald Broom GRA.

This picture was specially painted to show the red and green liveries. Other elements in it are based on the best available evidence but some are conjectural.

41

5

LOCOMOTIVES

by **Edward Talbot**

Introduction

When the LNWR was formed in July 1846, its three constituent companies became 'divisions' of the new company. The Grand Junction Railway, which had absorbed the Liverpool & Manchester Railway in 1845, became the Northern Division; the Manchester & Birmingham Railway became the Manchester & Birmingham Division, being renamed the North Eastern Division in 1849, when the lines between Manchester and Leeds were opened; and the London & Birmingham Railway became the Southern Division. Each division had its own locomotive department. The Northern Division headquarters were at Crewe, where the GJR had built a new works in 1843 to replace its previous establishment at Edge Hill, and its Superintendent of the Locomotive Engine Department was Francis Trevithick; he was assisted by Alexander Allan as Foreman of the Locomotives. The North Eastern Division works were at Longsight where John Ramsbottom was Locomotive Superintendent, and the Southern Division headquarters were at Wolverton, where James Edward McConnell was in charge, also with the title of Locomotive Superintendent.

No attempt was made to centralise responsibility for locomotive matters or even to introduce a measure of standardisation between divisions. Each divisional locomotive department pursued its own independent policy, much as it had done before the amalgamation. This situation merely reflected the position on the board of directors. As yet, the battle for control between the representatives of the constituent companies was unresolved. The GJR and L&BR in particular were uneasy bedfellows, and for years the rivalry and bickering between them centred on the locomotive departments, each superintendent having his own supporters among the directors. Indeed, there could have been no greater contrast than that between the designs of Crewe and Wolverton. Only when the opportunity presented itself, by a shift of power among the directors or the retirement of a superintendent, was any move made to centralise locomotive affairs.

The first change occurred in 1857 when Trevithick retired. John Ramsbottom was transferred to Crewe to be Locomotive Superintendent of the Northern Division, which henceforth took over the North Eastern Division also; the works at Longsight then ceased to be a divisional works but became more an adjunct of the running shed. Finally, in 1862 Admiral Moorsom, an old Southern Division supporter among the directors, died, Richard Moon became chairman, and his protégé, John Ramsbottom, was appointed Locomotive Superintendent of the entire system. McConnell had resigned shortly before. Henceforth all locomotive work was concentrated on Crewe, and Wolverton became the company's carriage works, though it continued to repair locomotives until 1877.

Detailed information about the early liveries used by the divisions is not available. All three divisions painted their engines green but there were differences in the shade of green and in the lining. From 1847, and probably well before, Crewe employed a livery of 'medium green' with black lining. Wolverton engines were a brighter shade of green and contrary to popular belief only one or two were painted red at the very end of McConnell's superintendence, perhaps as a last act of defiance to Crewe. After 1862 the Northern Division's green livery with black lining became standard for all LNWR engines, until Francis William Webb took over as Locomotive Superintendent in 1871.

Shortly afterwards a black livery was adopted, on the direct instruction, it is often stated, of the General Manager, William Cawkwell. A number of experimental schemes must have appeared at this time but unfortunately full details of them are not available. However, the scheme which was soon adopted was followed for the rest of the company's existence, and was later revived by British Railways. Passenger engines were painted glossy black, lined out in red, cream (often described as 'white') and grey, and goods engines were plain black. At first the lining was applied on some engines in a rather complicated way but on Webb's own engines a simpler form was evolved and this was soon applied throughout. From the middle of 1878 passenger engines were adorned with the coat of arms and from the early 1890s many goods engines were fully lined out also, like passenger engines but without the coat of arms.

Webb retired in 1903 and was replaced by George Whale, who in turn was succeeded by C.J.Bowen Cooke in 1909, but neither of these engineers made any basic changes in the livery scheme of the late Webb period. In 1914 all lining out ceased, as an economy measure during the First World War, but was resumed, for passenger engines only, in late 1921, just before the company's amalgamation with the Lancashire & Yorkshire Railway. Goods engines were never again lined out after the war, though of course some which had been lined out previously were still in service up to the end of the company's existence.

Southern Division

For almost the whole of its existence the Southern Division continued to use the green livery it had inherited from the London & Birmingham Railway in 1846, at first with the same black bands but later with other styles of lining. The livery had been adopted by Edward Bury, who had first been appointed 'contractor for locomotives' by the L&BR in July 1835 but became Locomotive Superintendent two years later when the contractor system broke down. The locomotive committee of the board of directors took decisions from the outset on such things as the design of engine numberplates and presumably liveries. Unfortunately, the minutes and other archives contain virtually nothing on the subject. Information on the L&BR liveries comes mainly from surviving illustrations and drawings, published accounts and various other sources.

In 1841 Charles Dickens described a London & Birmingham engine as having 'a shiny green and gold back, like an unpleasant beetle', which is probably a good account of the general effect. In detail, the livery of Bury's four-wheeled engines, based on published sources and old illustrations, was as follows: the boiler, wheels, tender, footplate sidesheets, wooden lagging on the lower part of the firebox, the bufferbeam ends, and perhaps the front also, were all painted green; the smokebox, chimney, boiler cleading bands, lining on the tender frame and in three oblong panels on the tender side, and the tender axle-guards, were black; the domed firebox sheathing was polished copper; and the splashers, safety-valve casings and smokebox door frame were polished brass. The engine number was displayed on the chimney front, on an elliptical brass plate on the boiler side, and on the tender frame.

By the late 1840s the black panels on the tender side, and perhaps on the back also, had reversed corners, and some footplate side-sheets and outside cylinders had panels with reversed corners too. Two drawings by E.T.Lane in 1849, of engines at this period, have survived. One shows 6'0" 2-2-2 No. 12, built by Bury, Curtis & Kennedy in September 1848. The boiler, wheels, side-sheet, lower firebox lagging, bufferbeam end, and perhaps the front, are painted green; the bar frame, boiler cleading bands, smokebox and chimney are black; the firebox top and chimney cap are polished copper; and the safety-valve cover,

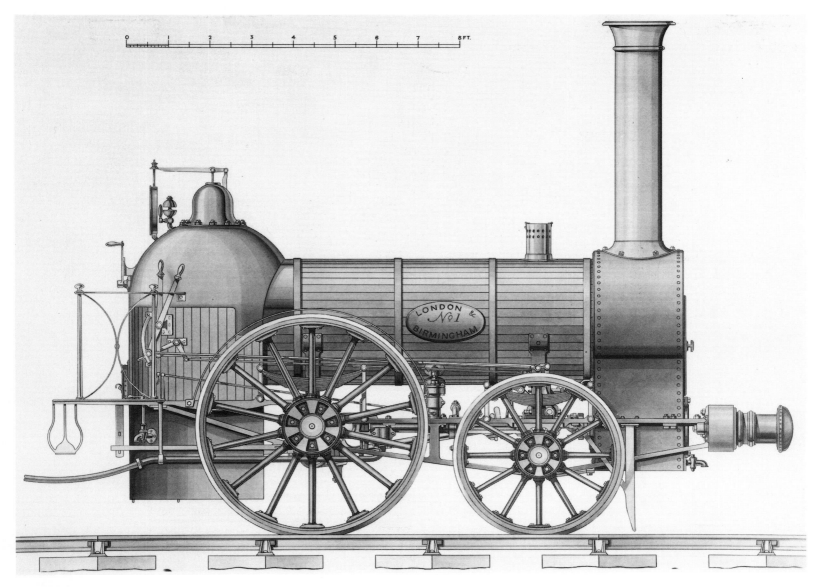

splasher, ring between smokebox and boiler, and the axle end (Bury's works plate) are polished brass.

The other drawing is of the 8′0″ Crampton, No. 245 LIVERPOOL, built by Bury, Curtis & Kennedy in October 1848. This has the boiler, outside cylinder, splasher, regulator box on the top of the boiler, and lower firebox lagging, all green; the boiler bands, wheels, outside frame, smokebox, chimney and the inside of the splasher are black; the firebox top and steam pipes are copper; and the safety-valve cover, axleboxes and axle end are brass. The nameplate is of brass with black serif capitals. A later drawing of LIVER-POOL in 1851, in black and white, shows an LNWR coat of arms on the cylinder. It seems to be the design used later for carriages rather than the one adopted for locomotives by Webb in 1878, which may well indicate that the drawing was done much later and without proper information.

All available evidence for the McConnell period up to 1861 indicates a green livery but with variations in the lining on certain engines. Photographs of No. 35 (Sharp single), No. 189 (Jones & Potts long-boiler single) and No. 236 (Wolverton 0−4−2) appear to show plain dark boiler bands; no lining can be seen on the engines but No. 189's tender has dark lines forming panels with reversed corners. The livery in all these cases seems to be green with black lining. Domes, safety-valve covers and splasher rims are polished brass. No. 189 seems to have a copper top to the chimney but the others seem to have painted tops.

The actual green would appear to have been a middle, slightly bluish shade, like the

Figure 6 *(G.H.Platt collection)*
Standard Bury passenger engine of the London & Birmingham Railway as built in the late 1830s.

Southern Railway's malachite green. This is on the evidence of paint taken from McConnell-style tender frames on the Cromford & High Peak line in 1967. They still had, beneath a layer of pitch, their successive coats of paint. Under Webb's black were two or more layers of green but they were all of the same shade, indicating no change between earlier paintings, presumably by the Southern Division, and later paintings, presumably in Northern Division green. In the locomotive committee minutes between January 1850 and April 1853 the purchase of large quantities of black and green paint is regularly recorded. The green paint is sometimes described as 'Brunswick' or 'Light Brunswick' green. Brunswick green is again mentioned in September 1856. In July 1857 there is a note about a test with green paint, comparing paint ground in oil with paint ground dry.

McConnell's 7′6″ 'Patent' class singles appeared amid a lot of publicity in November 1852 and appropriately had a much more elaborate livery scheme, so far as can be deduced from drawings. The side-sheets and tender sides are lined in panels having corners with three steps. This stepped-corner lining can be seen in a very early photograph of 'Bloomer' No. 249 as built in October 1851, that is, without weather board and extra lock-up safety valves, and also in drawings of long-boiler goods engines No. 281, built in July 1854, and No. 321, built in February 1855. Very similar, perhaps identical, lining can be seen on an 0−4−2 tank built in 1859 for the Leeds, Bradford & Halifax Railway by Kitson. This firm had built McConnell express goods engines for the Southern Division in 1854.

Yet another style of lining is shown in the well known photograph of 'Small Bloomer' No. 103, built in May 1857. The tender and side-sheet are lined in dark and light tones, in such a way as to suggest a panel with reversed corners on a dark surround with a raised rectangular frame. The actual colours of this scheme are not known but as a guess the engine was green with lining in some shades of red and yellow. This livery is probably the one described by Frank S.Hennell on the 'Bloomers': 'bright green with red and yellow lines; some of McConnell's large express engines . . . had their bufferbeams painted green with a panel in red and yellow lines in the same style as the side-sheets and tender tanks

45

Plate 55 *(E. Talbot collection)*
Probably the earliest surviving photograph of a 'Bloomer' is this fine view of 'Small Bloomer' No. 103, which was built at Wolverton in May 1857, the photograph probably being taken not long afterwards. Clearly, the livery is Southern Division green, though the lining is open to speculation.

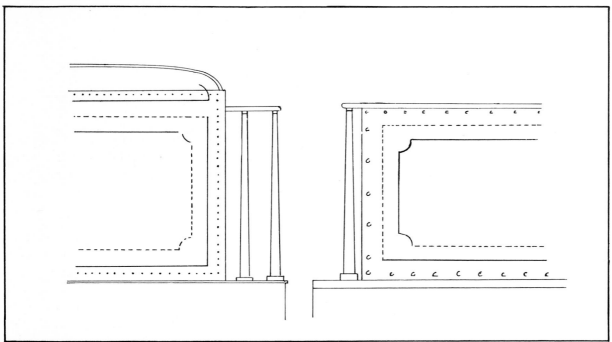

Figure 7 *(Alan Gettings)*
Drawing showing the arrangement of lining on No. 103. The continuous line is possibly yellow, or at least some light colour, such as cream, grey or white; the broken line is red and so has barely been recorded on the emulsion.

of those engines'. They were 'without exception the handsomest of engines when running'. Other sources show a rectangular panel between the buffers on 'Patent' No. 297, built in November 1852.

All the evidence up to this point indicates the use of a green livery. This may be disappointing in the light of all that has been written about McConnell's big red engines and the fine paintings of Cramptons and 'Bloomers' in scarlet or vermilion. But despite a prolonged search, no contemporary evidence of a red livery, or indeed of anything other than green, has been found. Unfortunately, no description exists of McConnell's 'H' class, or 'Extra Large Bloomer', No. 373, which was exhibited at the International Exhibition of 1862; the only photograph shows the engine in works grey. However, a photograph of 'Small Bloomer' No. 381 taken at the same time, December 1861, shows a new engine fully painted. The ground colour appears very dark, and in view of the characteristics of the 'ordinary' photographic plates then in use, can only have been red; but whether it is vermilion or a darker shade, it is impossible to say. The lining is again different. As on No. 103, there is a recessed panel effect, with reversed corners, but the arrangement of light and dark lines is different; there is an extra light line, unshaded, within the panels, and an elaborate Stroudley-style lining outside the boiler bands. This lining was perhaps in black, white and grey. This then is the first real evidence of red livery,

46

Plate 56 *(G.H.Platt collection)*

The only known photograph of a Southern Division engine in red livery, 'Small Bloomer' No. 381 at Wolverton, presumably in December 1861 on completion.

only months before the end of the Southern Division's independence.

About a year earlier, on 10th January 1861, McConnell reported to the stores committee that he had been 'trying a metallic oxide paint from Messrs Foulger & Sons which answers and is more economical'. This may well be a reference to the new red colour scheme, as the same sort of description, 'oxide of iron', was used by the Midland Railway of its own red livery, adopted on grounds of economy in 1883. It may also date the introduction of a red livery by McConnell fairly precisely, in which case it may be assumed that only a small number of engines had been so painted before the green livery of Crewe was applied to the Southern Division engines.

After Ramsbottom took over, the Southern Division engines were painted in the same livery as those of the Northern Division, which in most cases was probably no great change. Clement E.Stretton makes no mention of any change of colour when he records that in 1862 'the chimney tops and domes of all the McConnell engines were painted over to save the trouble of cleaning'. This is confirmed by photographs of Southern Division engines in Ramsbottom livery, which show all-over green paint, safety valves included. The Southern Division Sharp singles on the Euston to Watford and St.Albans trains are described by Rosling Bennett: 'They all had a graceful outline, but were not assisted in any way by the painter's art, the colour being a uniform dull green, boiler, frames, splashers, domes and everything except the safety-valve cover, which was invariably left bright.'

Engine Numbers

From 1837 to 1862 the London & Birmingham and Southern Division engines carried their numbers on the front of the chimney in cut-out brass numerals, latterly in a bold square-serif style. The first railway to put the engine number in this position was the Liverpool & Manchester, and the practice later spread to many lines, such as the MSLR, the Metropolitan and the New South Wales Railway of Australia, where many McConnell features long outlived their Wolverton prototype. Pictures of the mid-fifties also show the number on the back of the tender tank but this position may well have been used from Bury's day.

From 1856 the number was painted on the engine bufferbeam, in numerals of the same size and style as those on the chimney. This originated when the locomotive stock was partially renumbered. The new number was painted on the bufferbeam in readiness for the change, and on the morning of the 1st April 1856 the number on the chimney was blacked out, to be replaced by the new number at the earliest convenient time. According to the article in *The Locomotive Magazine* which recorded this (Vol 3, 1898, page 6), the numbers on the bufferbeam were then painted out; but this must be wrong. On all known photographs showing the front of a Southern Division engine the number is painted between the buffers. Moreover, the entry in the Sharp Stewart order book for 'Bloomers' Nos. 399-403, delivered in October and November 1861, reads: 'Nos. to be painted upon the buffer plank of Engines'. The painted numerals were shaded to the right and below with a darker colour, and the bufferbeam was edged with an inch-wide dark band. These features, and the treatment of 'N°', which differed from the Crewe style under Ramsbottom, can best be seen in the photograph of No. 35.

From 1837 to 1846 an elliptical brass numberplate was fixed centrally on the boiler side. The words 'LONDON &' were curved above the cut-down serif numerals and 'BIRMINGHAM' below. On the earlier engines the numerals were preceded by 'No.'. These plates were discontinued on the formation of the LNWR in July 1846, although No. 102, built earlier that year, still had its plates in January 1850. Thereafter the number was painted in serif numerals on the side of the boiler, usually in the middle but sometimes at the front. Nos. 176-181, Tayleur long-boiler singles of March and April 1847, had their numbers on the side of the dome. Strangely, no photograph records a number painted on the side of an engine. Perhaps they were discontinued when the bufferbeam numbers were introduced.

The engine number was also displayed on the tender frame. In 1837 a circular cast-iron numberplate, flanked by the shields of London and Birmingham, was fixed on the centre of the tender sole bar. The shields were presumably painted in their heraldic colours. These plates also probably disappeared in 1846. In the fifties the number was painted in small numerals on the tender frame. Similar small numerals were painted on each wheel centre, with the suffix 'L' on the leading and 'T' on the trailing wheel. These can be seen in photographs of Nos. 103, 249 and 381.

Engines of McConnell's own design were fitted with numberplates of various sorts. The 'Patent' class had a big elliptical plate on the side-sheet, the 'Large Bloomers', the 'Extra Large Bloomers' and the later 'Small Bloomers' had similar but smaller plates. The earlier 'Small Bloomers' had a plate shaped like a keystone at the top of the splasher. No. 227 ('Mac's Mangle') of December 1848 and No. 371, express goods of 1861, were numbered on the coupling-rod splasher of the middle wheel. The Stothert and Fairbairn long-boiler goods possibly had elliptical plates on the side-sheets. In each case, the lettering was different in style, wording and arrangement, and in view of the very small number of available photographs, it is likely that other, unrecorded varieties existed.

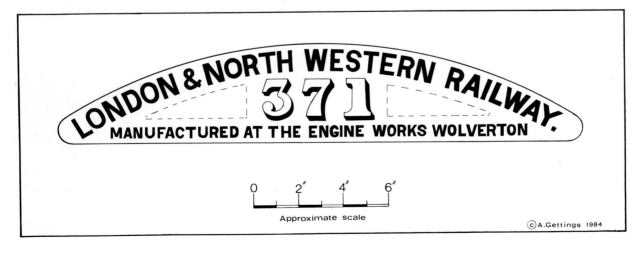

Figure 8 *(Alan Gettings)* Drawing of the Southern Division numberplate carried on the coupling-rod splasher of 0-6-0 No. 371, based on the evidence of a photograph. The contents of the etched areas are uncertain but seem to be either scrolls or a heraldic motif, perhaps incorporating the company's initials.

48

Brightwork

Most engines had plenty of polished metal about them. Bury's fireboxes, whether of the haystack variety or the normal type (as on his 6′ 2−2−2 of 1848), were covered with a sheet of polished copper. Brass domes and safety-valve casings were almost universal, although the extra lock-up valve fitted by McConnell from the mid-fifties was normally painted. Bury's splashers were brass, and McConnell perpetuated this with a broad double brass edging on the splashers of his passenger engines. The corniced dome of polished brass was a McConnell trademark; an example survives on the preserved engine in Sydney, Australia.

Copper chimney caps were fitted to Bury engines built from 1845, that is: Nos. 59, 60, 91, 93, 94, and 96-118. Works drawings of the Bury singles of 1848 and of the Vulcan Foundry 'Small Bloomers', Nos. 310-3, of 1854 show copper-capped chimneys. Despite this, and other reports that McConnell engines had copper caps, they cannot be seen in photographs. Though it may be that the old photographic emulsion translated the red tinge of the copper into black, nevertheless the chimney caps themselves do not look shiny.

Nameplates

McConnell reputedly had an antipathy to names on engines, and his own engines certainly ran nameless during his regime. The only named engines on the line were those which were inflicted on him by the board despite his protests, the Cramptons LONDON and LIVERPOOL, those belonging to the permanent-way department and those transferred from Crewe, from other divisions or from absorbed railways.

Except for the Crewe engines, all nameplates seem to have been fitted to the boiler side. According to the drawing of LIVERPOOL, the nameplates were of brass with black serif capitals. They were apparently transferred to express goods No. 245, built in April 1859, which was considered a rebuild of the Crampton! The twenty-nine South Staffordshire Railway engines which were absorbed in 1858 all bore names (one was McCONNELL); according to the Leitch drawing in *The Locomotive Magazine*, the lettering was in large sansserif capitals. The names were still in use in June 1859 but may have been taken off when the engines were renumbered into Southern Division stock in that year.

In January 1860 the working of the Trent Valley line was transferred from the Northern Division to the Southern Division, and thirty-two Crewe engines with names such as OSTRICH and OWL came under Wolverton's control. Ramsbottom asked the stores committee if the nameplates could be returned and, according to legend, McConnell had them loaded into a wagon, marked boldly: 'Trash — for Crewe'.

Northern Division 1846-1862: LNWR 1862-1871

Details of the locomotive livery applied in the earliest days of Crewe are not well documented but the green livery which was standard in Ramsbottom's time is believed to date back to the formation of the LNWR and may well have been the original colour of Grand Junction Railway engines. Certainly it was applied to the Crampton engine, No. 176 COURIER, which was completed at Crewe in November 1847, though the livery of the detail parts of the engine is open to doubt. A painting by E.W.Twining, reproduced in A.R.Bennett's *Historic Locomotives and Moving Accidents*, shows the whole engine and tender green, including the bufferbeams and wheel centres; only the tyres, buffers and smokebox are painted black. Another source says that there was a white diamond in the centre of the bufferbeams.

Fortunately, better information is available about the green livery of the Ramsbottom era from the handful of photographs which have survived showing engines in this livery. Nevertheless, complete details of the painting scheme of all classes are not known. The photographs fall into two groups. Firstly, there are a number of pictures showing engines as running in everyday service. All these show black lining, and among them must be included the well known view of LADY OF THE LAKE by the clock tower of the Old

49

Works at Crewe. The second group consists of five photographs, all taken at the Old Works, but showing white lining of a much more complicated kind than appears in any photograph of black lining. There is no evidence that white lining was ever used in service and it is clear that it was only applied for photographic purposes, so that the lining would stand out on the relatively insensitive photographic emulsions of the day. It served this purpose excellently; but it has also led some observers to the mistaken conclusion that it in fact formed part of the Ramsbottom livery (as well as to the incorrect painting of Ramsbottom 0−4−0ST No. 1439, currently preserved at the National Railway Museum).

The five photographs showing white lining are of 'Problem' No. 565, the 2−4−0s SAMSON and NEWTON, 'DX' No. 568 STEWART and 0−4−0ST No. 1437. The best ex-

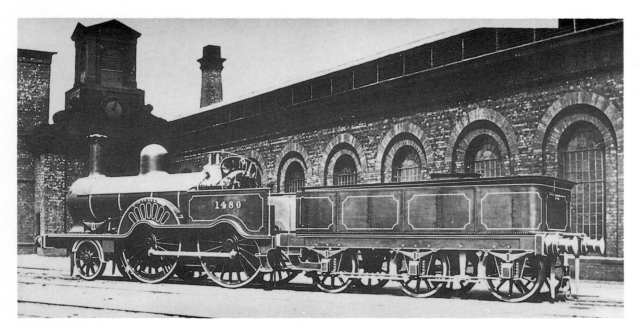

Plate 57 *(G.H.Platt collection)*
Ramsbottom 2−4−0 No. 1480 NEWTON outside the Old Works at Crewe with white lining of a far more complicated kind than can be seen in any photograph of a green engine in ordinary service. The engine is probably new, in which case the date is April 1866.

ample is perhaps that of NEWTON, which shows the lining on the engine boiler, splashers, footplate side sheets and tender sides and rear, very clearly as it was applied in black; but in addition all the tyres have been painted white and there is complicated lining of the leading wheel spring and splasher, the cab footsteps, the tender springs and axleboxes, the bufferbeam ends and buffer housings. Of these only the splasher of the leading wheel had any lining in reality.

The general effect of these photographs is quite striking and is in some contrast with the actual livery of Ramsbottom's day, which was rather plain if not austere. The green itself is variously described as 'medium green', 'medium green with a slight tendency to blue' and 'a deep chrome green'. From paint scraped from the Ramsbottom 0−4−0ST and examined by ICI paint experts, it is believed to have corresponded to British Standard BS381C of 1964 'brilliant green'. This green is believed to have been applied to the whole engine, including the bufferbeams and wheels, only the tyres and smokebox being black. A single black band, approximately $\frac{3}{4}''$ wide as nearly as can be judged from available sources, was the only lining. On footplate side panels the line was $4\frac{1}{2}''$ from the edge, with reversed corners of $4''$ or $4\frac{1}{2}''$ radius. A black band ran along the inner edge of the peripheral beading on the splashers and their radial slots were similarly edged with black. The boiler cleading bands had a $\frac{1}{2}''$ black line along each edge. On the 'DX' class the coupling rod splashers also had the lined beading but the openings in the splashers, so far as can be judged from photographs, did not have black edging.

This was the livery as applied to tender engines of Ramsbottom's own design but all tender engines were basically painted in the same way, with variations to suit the design features of individual classes. For instance, the various Trevithick 'Old Crewe' types had footplate side panels made up of three separate plates, the centre one displaying the engine

50

Plate 58 *(G.H.Platt collection)*

The earliest known view of a 'Problem', No. 229 WATT at Preston in the early 1880s. It is in original condition, with small sandbox, no injectors, an early type of nameplate showing the name only, and a 2000-gallon tender. The lining can be seen on the tender and partly on the side-sheet but virtually nowhere else, as the engine is so dirty — streaks of dirt have run down from the splasher slots and the number has been wiped clean.

Plate 59 *(G.H.Platt collection)*

'Newton' No. 1745 JOHN BRIGHT in ordinary service in the early 1870s. This photograph gives a good idea of the plain austere effect of the green livery used for the whole of the LNWR from 1862 to 1873.

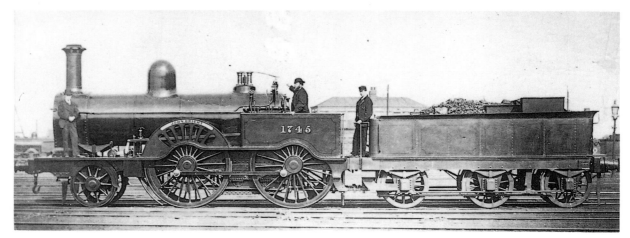

Plate 60 *(G.H.Platt collection)*

'Newton' No. 1746 BEVERE (named after Sir Richard Moon's house in Worcestershire) at Patricroft in the early 1870s.

51

number. Each of these plates had a tall narrow panel in the same style as the single panel on the side-sheet of a Ramsbottom engine. The Trevithick engines also had sandboxes on the driving wheel splashers and these too had a simple black panel, without reversed corners, following the shape of the sandbox, the inner line being curved to complement the splasher.

Some sources indicate that the panels were delineated not with a single black line but with two black lines, the outer one being thicker than the inner one. This may well have been so in the early days but the only known photograph showing such lining is that of LADY OF THE LAKE outside the Old Works and it appears on the tender only. Possibly, this lining was specially used on this engine for the 1862 International Exhibition.

The Ramsbottom six-wheel tenders had the sides lined out to form four panels, following the joints in the plates; each panel was in the same style and to the same specification

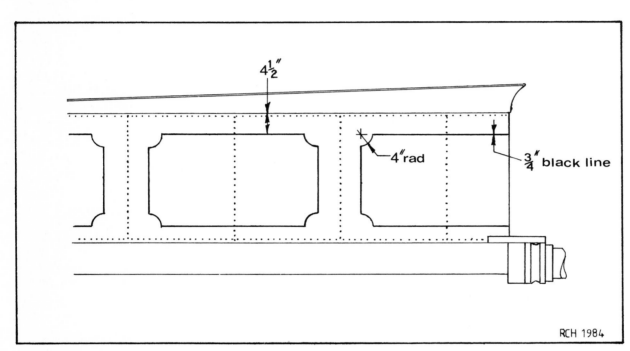

RCH 1984

Figure 9 *(R.C.Hunt)*
Drawing of typical black lining on a Ramsbottom tender in the green livery.

as the side panel on the engine footplate. Ramsbottom tenders had rounded front and rear corners, and so the front and rear panels were carried round these corners, the rear one leading to a single panel on the back of the tender. In the 'white lining' photograph of the 'DX' STEWART, completed in August 1861, there is a white diamond in the centre of the rear panel. Clearly, at some stage these white diamonds were a regular feature of the LNWR livery; they were derived from the Egyptian diamond of the Grand Junction Railway and served to denote company ownership, like a modern trademark or 'logo'.

No photographs are of sufficiently good quality to show the lining on four-wheel tenders. But most probably they were lined in the same style as six-wheel tenders: the panels would match the joints in the plates and would be carried round the corners, the lower line being 'lost' under the rear toolbox, where fitted. Certain four-wheeled tenders, as on Southern Division engines, had square corners and were lined in flat panels like the side tanks of tank engines.

Tank engines were lined in much the same way as tender engines, though no photograph exists of a 'Special Tank' in green and only a 'white lining' photograph survives of an 0 – 4 – 0ST. The latter shows that the footplate side panel was lined in one panel as on a Ramsbottom tender engine; but the rear sheet to the footplate on these engines had a large opening, to facilitate firing, and has two tall narrow panels, one on either side. These panels are adapted to suit the shape of the sides, which are not symmetrical. 'Special Tanks' did not have this feature and so would have had one panel in the usual style. The 0 – 4 – 0ST picture also shows lining on the boiler cleading bands beneath the tank, which

52

would also be expected. Unfortunately, no photograph exists to give any indication of how the tank itself was lined. In the black livery scheme of Webb's day the saddle tank was treated as one large panel and this may well have been so with the green livery also. Side-tank engines, such as the Trevithick 'Old Crewe' $2-4-0$Ts, had panels on the tank sides conforming to the separate plates, as on tender engines. The bunkers of these engines, and of other tank engines such as those converted from Sharp $2-2-2$ tender engines by the North Eastern Division, had tall narrow panels to suit.

The engine number was displayed on the cab side-sheet, or on the side tank of some tank engines, in either yellow or gold leaf, shaded in black. It was also displayed on the front bufferbeams of tender engines and on both front and rear bufferbeams of tank engines. In both cases 'N°' appeared to the left of the drawhook and the number to the right (looking at the front of the engine). A number of photographs seem to have the number enclosed in a black panel, in the same style as was standard on the red bufferbeams used later in the black livery.

In the early days all Northern Division engines were named but Ramsbottom ceased naming goods engines in 1859-62. Engines which were not named had numberplates, in the same style as nameplates, on the centre splashers. This was discontinued in 1872; a

Figure 10 *(Alan Gettings)* Numerals as used on the splasher numberplates of some Ramsbottom engines.

note from the works manager dated 25th March states: 'In future all engines which have no names will not require a numberplate on wheel cover. The number and date can be stamped neatly on the Regulator quadrant.' Classes built after this date were the 'DX' $0-6-0$s and the 'Special Tanks'. No photograph exists showing one of these numberplates on a 'Special Tank', $0-4-0$ST or on one of the 'Problems' which were not named on first completion. A 'white lining' photograph of one of the latter, No. 565, built in May 1861, shows no such splasher numberplate.

Shed plates at this period were fixed on the rear side of the weatherboard, in the centre of the top edge, and had white letters on a dark ground. An example can be clearly seen in the photograph of LADY OF THE LAKE outside the Old Works. Tender numberplates are thought to have been unchanged in style throughout the company's history and to have been black with letters and numbers picked out in white.

In general, by comparison with other railways' engines, there was little brightwork at this period. The brass safety valve columns of Ramsbottom valves, and of those on Trevithick engines, were polished, as were the exposed copper parts of Trevithick fireboxes, Ramsbottom's castellated chimney tops and, no doubt, certain cab fittings. But domes were painted and the rectangular-section coupling rods of the day were invariably black, perhaps painted or perhaps blackened chemically in some way. Outside connecting rods, however, as on Trevithick engines and the 'Problems', were finished bright.

The Transition to Black 1871-1873

John Ramsbottom retired as Locomotive Superintendent on 1st October 1871 and was succeeded by F.W.Webb. A month later, on 2nd November, the first engine to be painted black was turned out of Crewe Works. It was No.2045, the first of Webb's 'Special Tanks'. Whether it was lined or not is uncertain but most probably it was plain black; certainly it was experimental, as engines continued to be outshopped in green for some time, the last to be so painted not being turned out until April 1873. So during this period of about eighteen months the new black livery was evolved. Exactly how this occurred is not well documented. But enough photographs have survived to enable part of the story at least to be pieced together.

The first discernible changes took place with engines in the green livery. A number can be seen with the livery as before except that the lining of the panels on the footplate side-sheets and tender has rounded corners instead of reversed. These changes can be assumed to have occurred under Webb, as the engines also have Webb chimneys instead of the Ramsbottom castellated type. Examples of engines in this livery include two Ramsbottom 'Newtons' and two Southern Division tank engines. The latter would probably have been shopped by Crewe at this time and were not likely to have been the sort of engines which would have been experimented on. It may be reasonably deduced therefore that this change was applied to all engines painted green at this period. One of the 'Newtons', No. 1684 SPEKE, clearly has a red bufferbeam with a black line forming a rectangular panel, as later became standard, black edging to the bufferbeam and black buffer housings. But it has no bufferbeam number, contrary to what would be expected on a green engine. So it would appear that the black panel from the green bufferbeam of Ramsbottom's time was retained when the colour of the bufferbeam was changed to red. This may have been experimental on this engine only; or, more probably, was another change in the green livery at this time. The date of this photograph, as determined by various fittings on the engine, would be about 1875 but the repainting must have been done before then. Another possibility, of course, is that engines still in green all had their bufferbeams painted red for reasons of standardisation and safety.

What was perhaps the next stage is depicted in an ex works view of the first of the Webb 'Newtons', No. 1211 JOHN RAMSBOTTOM, which was completed in March 1872,

Plate 61 *(G.H.Platt collection)*
'Newton' No. 1684 SPEKE at Crewe shed (later known as Crewe North) about 1873, in original condition except for the Webb chimney and lamp socket at the top of the smokebox, introduced in 1872-3. The livery combines features of the Ramsbottom and Webb styles — the engine is green but the black lining has rounded corners, not reversed, and the bufferbeam is red with a black rectangular centre panel and no number, as used on black engines later. The date when red bufferbeams were introduced is not known.

with open splashers but Webb cab and chimney. It is a broadside view, so the bufferbeam is not visible, and it is not possible to be certain about the colours of the engine; but it seems to show a green engine, with painted numbers and black tyres as in the standard green livery, but lined out in red, cream and grey in the style which was first used on black engines (that is, with red, cream and grey on the boiler cleading bands as well as elsewhere).

Though No.1211 was numerically the first of the batch, it was not the first to be out-shopped, perhaps because of its experimental livery, though the second of the batch also had a different livery. An article by S.S.Scott in *Loco News and Railway Contractor*, page 59, Vol XI (1922) states: 'No. 1212 PIONEER, the first passenger engine turned out by Webb, appeared in a very dark coloured paint, generally termed "invisible green". It looked like black, unless observed in a good light, when it could easily be seen that it was actually very dark green.' The next step would seem to have been to move to a black paint proper, combined with the lining of No. 1211. All that was then needed was to replace painted numbers with cast numberplates. Scott also states, in the same article, that 'DX' No. 1536 followed soon after in black, but green remained the standard colour until the advent of the 'Coal Engines'.

In this way, it may be assumed, the famous black livery was evolved. The first cast numberplate is known to have been made on 11th January 1873, presumably for the first of the '17″ Coal Engine' 0−6−0s, completed in February. It is also known that the last engine to be painted green was outshopped on 2nd April of that year and must have been No. 502, the eighth of the '17″ Coal Engines'. So the first eight of this class must have been alone in having the green livery with cast numberplates instead of painted numbers. Unfortunately, no photograph of one of them in this condition exists. Nor is it known how the numberplate was painted, possibly yellow numerals on a black ground. But the style of the numerals was clearly designed to perpetuate that of Ramsbottom's painted numbers. The ninth engine of the batch was turned out in the new standard plain black with cast numberplate.

The first passenger engine to appear in black lined red, cream and grey is not known; but one of the first, if not the first, must have been 'Problem' No. 806 WAVERLEY. A photograph exists showing this engine newly turned out of the works and temporarily renamed SHAH OF PERSIA in honour of the Shah's visit to Crewe Works in June 1873. The first new engines to receive the livery were almost certainly the last batch of Webb 'Newtons', the first of which, No. 1141 S.R.GRAVES, came out in August. Until the change to black was made in the first half of 1873, all engines put through the works were almost certainly repainted green. S.S.Scott records that except for the experimental PIONEER and the black 'DX' all engines were green in March 1872. Even after black was adopted for all repainting and new engines, many engines must have continued in green for some years. Not until March 1880 did *The English Mechanic* record: 'LNWR engines are now all painted black'.

Plate 63 *(G.H.Platt collection)*
Webb '17″ Coal Engine' No. 433, as built. On these, and all goods engines up to the early 1890s, the only relief from plain black was the red background to the numberplate and the red of the front bufferbeam.

Plate 64 *(G.H.Platt collection)*
The well known picture of 'Problem' No. 806 when temporarily renamed SHAH OF PERSIA in June 1873, on which occasion it is believed to have been the first engine to be painted black. The lining seen here is much more complicated than eventually became standard.

'Blackberry Black' 1873-1922

After 1873, with only two very special exceptions, all LNWR engines were painted black right up to the end of the company's existence. At first passenger engines were lined and goods engines were plain black. The passenger engines included the Trevithick 6' and 7' 'Old Crewe' singles, CORNWALL and the 2−4−0 side and saddle tanks rebuilt from Trevithick 'Old Crewe' 2−4−0 goods engines. The latter were usually painted plain black but one photograph, of No. 327, allegedly taken in 1885, shows lining on the footplate side-sheet and possibly elsewhere. It may have been specially painted for a local passenger working. As a general rule all engines had cast numberplates. The main exceptions were Trevithick engines, both 2−2−2s and 2−4−0s, on the duplicate list; these had painted numbers, which according to Ahrons in *The Railway Magazine*, March 1915, were yellow shaded blue. At some later stage duplicate list engines also had cast numberplates.

Passenger engines began to appear with the company's coat of arms on the driving splasher in June 1878. A report in *The English Mechanic* on 12th July stated that the 'Precedents' AMAZON, BALMORAL, METEOR and PENRITH BEACON had recently been turned out of Crewe Works so adorned after general overhaul. The first new engines to have the coat of arms on completion were the ten 'Precedents' built in August and September, beginning with No. 1173 THE AUDITOR. Other passenger engines received the coat of arms as they passed through works for general repair. 'Precursor' 2−4−0s, for instance, are recorded as being turned out with it in March 1880.

About 1881 the 'Special DX' class began to be lined, as were the '18″ Goods' from their introduction in 1880. Though classed as 'Express Goods', both these classes were really 'mixed traffic', being intended for passenger traffic also. The '18″ Goods' also had the coat of arms, thereby earning the nickname 'Crested Goods' or less formally 'Cauliflowers'. Goods and mineral engines proper, that is, those with 4'5½″ driving wheels, remained plain black until June 1890, when '17″ Coal Engine' No. 360, 'Coal Tank' No. 848 and 'Special Tank' No. 2141 were photographed fully lined. From about this time goods engines were lined as a matter of course, including all the 0−8−0s from their introduction in 1892-3. Some, however, were never lined, the Trevithick 2−4−0s (with one or two exceptions), many 'Special Tanks' used on goods shunting, and the 2'6″ well tanks.

Goods engines, however, even when lined did not carry the coat of arms, though two other mixed-traffic classes did, Webb's four-cylinder compound 'Bill Baileys' and Whale's '19″ Goods'. The only tank engines which had it were: the three-cylinder compound 2−2−4−0T No. 777, which was specially finished for display at the Manchester Jubilee Exhibition in May-October 1887; EUSTON and LIVERPOOL, the two 'Special Tanks' converted for working passenger trains to Liverpool (Riverside); and the two large passenger tank classes of the twentieth century, Whale's 'Precursor Tanks' and Bowen Cooke's 4−6−2Ts. The official photograph of the first of the square saddle tank 0−4−2Ts of 1896, No. 317, shows the coat of arms but it is thought to have been applied for the photograph only. It cannot be seen in any photograph of the class in traffic.

All lining ceased at Crewe soon after war broke out in 1914. *The Locomotive Magazine* for 15th September 1914 states: 'Following on the declaration of war the paint shop at Crewe was practically depleted of all its engines, some being turned out with only one coat of paint and others that were ready for painting, etc.' Quite possibly no lining was done at all during the war, because of the extreme shortage of engines and the works' preoccupation with munitions and other war work. The last engine to be lined was 'Claughton' No. 250 J.A.BRIGHT and the first to be plain black was the next of the batch, No. 260 W.E.DORRINGTON, both being completed in August. Engines were then painted plain black as a matter of course, including the 1915 batch of 'George the Fifths', incidentally, not just the last one, DOVEDALE, as is commonly believed. The 'Princes' built in 1915 and later were also plain black but the twenty 'Princes' delivered from North British in 1915-6 were fully lined, as before the war, and were also named. Crewe also continued naming 'Claughtons', 'Princes' and 'Georges' until March 1917 when that too

57

ceased. The wartime livery was plain black with no lining and no coat of arms. In addition, many if not all engines were unvarnished also.

A minute of the Locomotive and Engineering Committee dated 20th October 1921 resolved: 'the pre-war practice of lining and varnishing engines, and of naming passenger engines, be resumed.' Some engines must have been so treated before the company merged with the LYR at the end of that year and in any case Crewe continued to turn engines out fully lined well into LMS days. Normally these engines had the coat of arms as before, along with many engines turned out in plain black at this period also, but one 'Claughton', No. 154, was unique about 1922 in having full lined livery but no coat of arms.

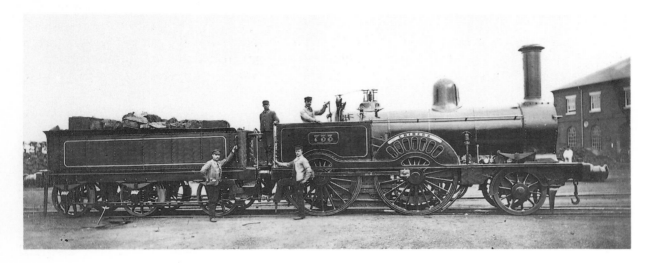

Plate 65 *(G.H.Platt collection)*
'Samson' No. 733 CHIMERA in original condition (even with its Giffard injector, indicated by the large handwheel for the steam supply on the side of the firebox) except for the Webb chimney. It has fully lined boiler bands and more lining on the tender frames than in the later standard scheme.

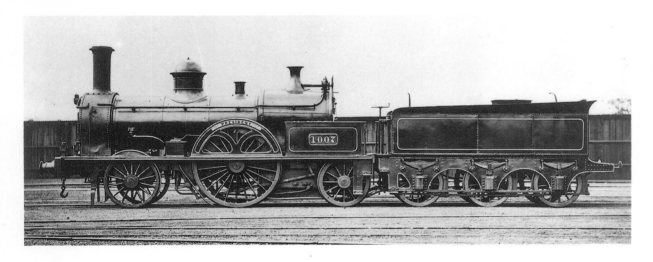

Plate 66 *(E.Dutton collection)*
'Large Bloomer' No. 1007 PRESIDENT in original condition except for its Webb chimney; the photograph was probably taken before scrapping in 1877. The lining is in the early style, being applied to the tender frames, and curving down at either end of the footplate edging. For some reason, there seems to be no lining on the boiler bands. The numberplate reads 'CREWE WORKS'!

Plate 67 *(E.Dutton collection)*
'Precedent' No. 2176 ROBERT BENSON, probably photographed on completion in February 1875. It has full lining on the boiler bands and on both sides of the tender frames, and the lining on the footplate edging curves downwards where it ends behind the front bufferbeam but not at the other end, where it curves round and down the outer edge of the dragbox.

Plate 68 *(G.H.Platt collection)*

Trevithick 2−4−0 tank No. 953 about 1880, with original boiler fittings but a Webb chimney, and in lined black livery with numberplates rather than painted numbers. There is lining along the lower edge of the frames, and round the opening for the slide bars, as well as on the sides of the tank and bunker. The connecting rod is bright and the coupling rod black, as normal. As a rule, tank engines were also lined on the rear of the bunker but no photograph of the rear of one of these engines, or of a 'Special Tank', is known, to confirm this.

Plate 69 *(E.Dutton collection)*

'Precedent' No. 1173 THE AUDITOR as completed in the final form of the black livery in August 1878 — two red lines on the boiler bands, coat of arms on the driving splasher, no lining on the lower edge of the tender frames, and lining on the footplate edging not curving down at the front (though it actually seems to curve down slightly before turning upwards at right angles behind the bufferbeam).

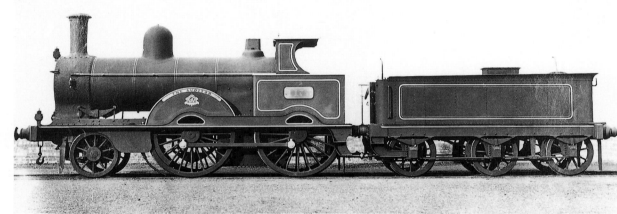

Plate 70 *(G.H.Platt collection)*

'Big Jumbo' No. 1485 SMEATON at Manchester London Road in the beautiful condition typical of the late 1880s. Handrails are finished bright but the coupling rods are black, being rectangular-section. The front coupling is the early type, with the shackle secured by a pin behind the hook, and there is no front vacuum hose, introduced in 1889.

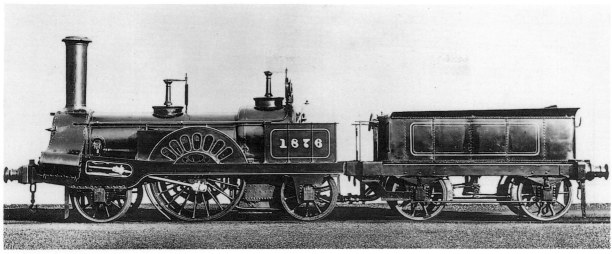

'Crewe Single' No. 1876 (formerly, No. 291 PRINCE OF WALES) in the black livery with painted numbers and probably red lines on the boiler bands. The lining on the tender frames curves down at both ends. The photograph may well have been taken before the engine became ENGINEER CREWE in 1879.

'Dreadnought' No. 637 CITY OF NEW YORK about 1890 in the standard black livery. These were the last class to have splashers for the leading wheels, with lining all round the outer edge. The connecting rods and slide bars are finished bright.

A rare rear view of 'Experiment' 2 – 2 – 2 – 0 No. 307 VICTOR at Shrewsbury about 1890 in the standard black livery. The rear of the tender is all black, including the bufferbeam, and though the tender numberplate has its figures and border picked out in white, they were very often all black too. Also clearly visible is the way the lining on the footplate edging of the engine curved round and vertically downwards across the end of the dragbox.

Plate 74 *(G.H.Platt collection)*

'Claughton' No. 154 CAP-TAIN FRYATT (named after the master of the GER steamer BRUSSELS, who was executed by the Germans for refusing to surrender to U-boats and open-ing fire instead) at Stalybridge about 1923. It is unique in hav-ing the full lined livery, resum-ed in late 1921, without the coat of arms on the splasher beneath the nameplate.

Colours of Paints

The black paint of an LNWR engine was officially specified as 'drop black'. The so-called 'blackberry black', though an excellent description of the overall effect was merely the combined result of drop black paint, varnish, the high finish attained and the conscien-tious work of the cleaners at the sheds. Many photographs, particularly of ex works engines, show a different finish on the smokebox. This is merely because of the absence of varnish on a part of the engine which frequently became very hot.

The lining colours of red, cream and grey are similarly descriptive of the lining as it appeared on the engines rather than of the paints used. An official specification supplied to the HMRS by British Railways in 1957 states: 'Lining grey, cream and vermilion all ready mixed purchased paints'. But even in late LNWR days all lining paints were mixed at Crewe, the red by the painters themselves and the other two colours by the paint mixers.

Examination of the preserved COLUMBINE and CORNWALL in the 1930s before their subsequent repaintings revealed that the grey line was in fact pale blue paint, to which subsequent varnishings had given the grey colour, the varnish itself being golden brown. Where the latter had worn off, on edges for example, the blue was quite obvious. The finished colour was described to G.H.Platt by a critical and contemporary observer as a 'blue-grey, not a grey-blue'. It was 'similar to dried lavender flowers seen in the mass, and was obtainable by mixing ultramarine blue, yellow ochre and crimson lake in flake white'. The cream line varied from off-white to a quite definitely orange-yellow tint, which could well have been white paint varnished, the appearance depending on the age of the varnish. In contemporary accounts it is often described as 'white', not cream, but the usual effect was that of very pale cream. It was described as 'flake white slightly tinted with yellow ochre'. The red is best described as scarlet rather than vermilion; not so yellow as vermilion and not so blue as crimson lake but a mixture of the two. It was the same shade as a ripe haw berry, the fruit of the common hawthorn or may tree.

Livery Details
General

On tender engines lining was applied to the cab panels, cab sides, boiler cleading bands and footplate edging, including coupling-rod splasher openings. There was no lining on sandboxes, wherever situated, footsteps, wheels or frames in general. On tank engines, the sides of the cab, tanks, and bunker, including the back of the bunker, were lined, together with the splashers, as on tender engines. On tenders, however, only the sides were lined; the back of the tender was plain black, including the bufferbeam, which was never red as on most railways. The footplate edging, or the wooden moulding on Webb tenders, was also lined as on the engines, and the frames of steel-framed tenders had their lower edges and cut-outs lined also.

The lining consisted of a broad grey line on the outside, a fine cream line on its inner edge, and a red line spaced a short distance away on the inside. The official thicknesses of these lines were: $\frac{5}{8}''$ for the grey, $\frac{1}{8}''$ for the cream and $\frac{1}{4}''$ for the red. Measurements on different engines and on large photographs have produced differing figures, and engines painted in postgrouping days have showed even greater variations, as do the preserved specimens. Consequently, in the figures which follow, more than one dimension is sometimes given.

Plate 75 (*E. Dutton collection*) 'Square saddle tank' No. 808 on completion in 1905 — the class was converted from '17″ Coal Engines'. The livery is in accordance with the principles that were then well established — boiler bands edged in red beneath the tank, splashers lined as for all goods engines with 4′5½″ wheels and no coat of arms, as a goods engine.

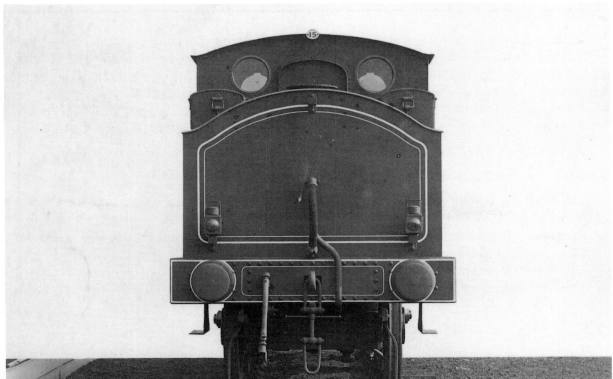

Plate 76 (*E. Dutton collection*) Rear of an '18″ Tank', showing how the lining followed the outline of the rear of the bunker and the rear bufferbeam was red and lined in the standard fashion.

Lining of panels

On panels in general (that is, cab panels, tank and tender sides, bunker sides and back) the grey line was $\frac{5}{8}''$ to $\frac{3}{4}''$ wide and was set in 5″ from the edges, except for the top line on tender sides, which was 3″ only from the lower edge of the coping. The cream line touching it was $\frac{1}{8}''$ wide, and spaced $1\frac{1}{2}''$ to $1\frac{5}{8}''$ away on the inside was the red line, $\frac{1}{4}''$ to $\frac{5}{16}''$ wide. At the corners the radius to the outside of the grey line was 4″, the red being concentric with it. On the upper part of the cab sides, the lining was only 3″ from the sides and roof angle, and $3\frac{1}{2}''$ from the bottom edge, because of the smaller space. The radii of the corners was also smaller, $1\frac{1}{2}''$ to the outside of the grey line and $\frac{3}{4}''$ to the red one. Saddle tanks were treated in the same way, the semi-circular tank being considered as a single panel. Square saddle tanks, which several classes had, were lined on the sides in the usual way for flat panels.

Figure 11(a) *(R.C.Hunt)*
Sketch showing general arrangement of lining on locomotives and positions of detail drawings of lining, (11b) opposite, of Diagram 1, boiler bands, opposite lower, and Diagram 2, splashers, page 65.

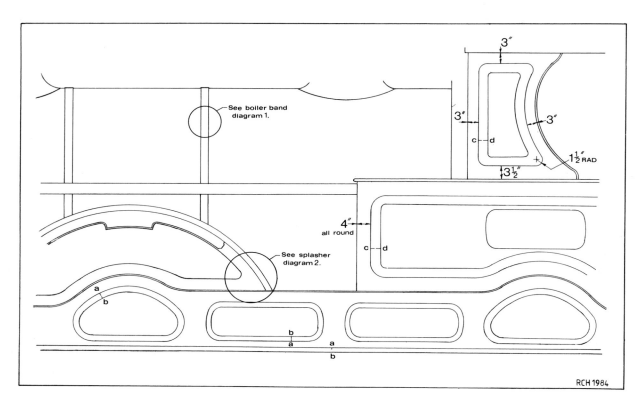

Boiler bands

Boiler cleading bands were at first given the full lining of red, cream and grey. In effect, there was a central line of red on the band, with lines of cream and grey on either side. From 1876 the boiler bands were lined with two parallel red lines only. The change is thought to have been made because the grey and cream lines discoloured with the heat of the boiler. This effect can be seen on certain photographs, which show the leading line on the band next to the smokebox to have been burnt almost entirely away.

Lining on Footplating

The footplate edging had a $\frac{5}{8}''$ grey line along the bottom edge with the usual $\frac{1}{8}''$ cream above it, and a $\frac{1}{4}''$ red line placed rather above the centre line of the edging; this was about $\frac{1}{2}''$ above the cream on engines with 2″ angle and $\frac{5}{8}''$ on the larger engines with $2\frac{1}{2}''$ angle. In the early days of the black livery, the lining curved downwards where it finished behind the front bufferbeam and also behind the rear drag box of engines designed before the '17″ Coal Engines' of 1873; this was similar to what was done later at the cab end of

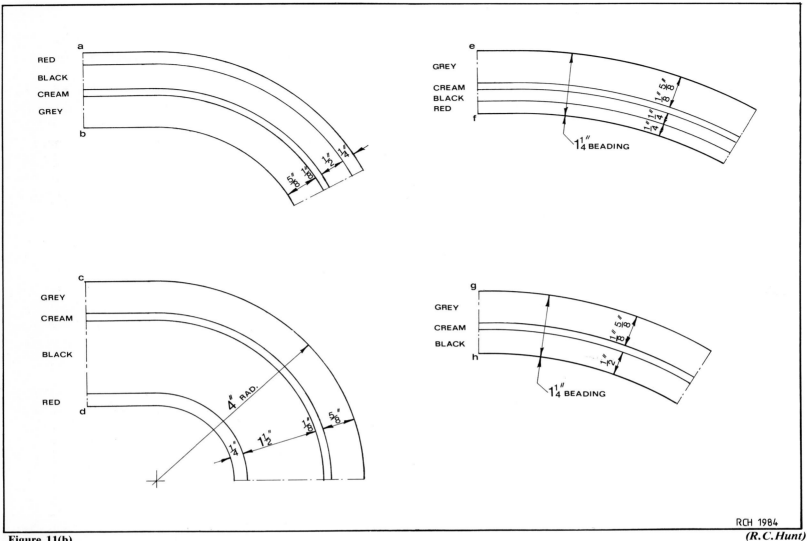

Figure 11(b)   *(R.C.Hunt)*
Detail drawings of lining at points shown in (11a) opposite, diagram 2 and Figure 12 on pages 65 and 66. Though the line widths of the various colours are all shown on curves for convenience, in practice the widths of lines in a-b and c-d applied only where the lines were straight; on curves they were 'swelled' slightly, otherwise they would have looked too narrow.

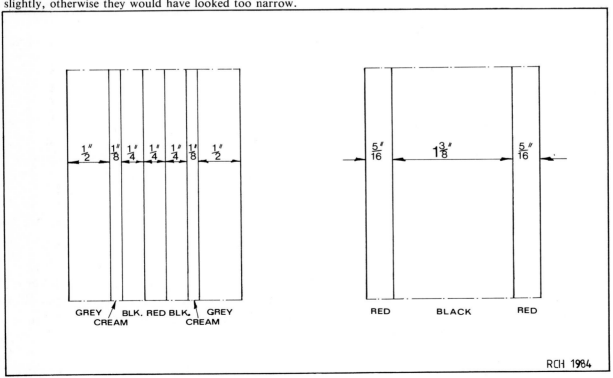

Diagram 1.
Lining on boiler bands: left, the pre-1876 full lining; right, the two red lines adopted in 1876.

Diagram 2.
Lining on splashers: above, on goods engines; below, on passenger engines. Detailed drawings of lining on the beading are shown in (11b), page 64.

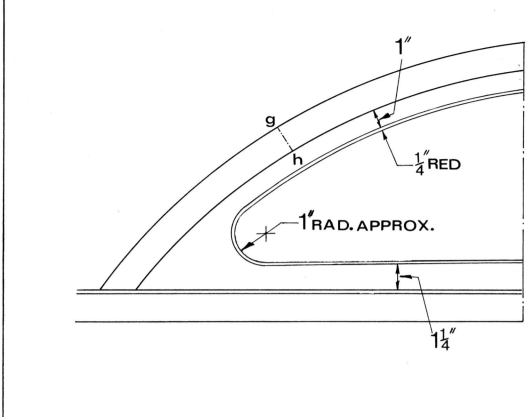

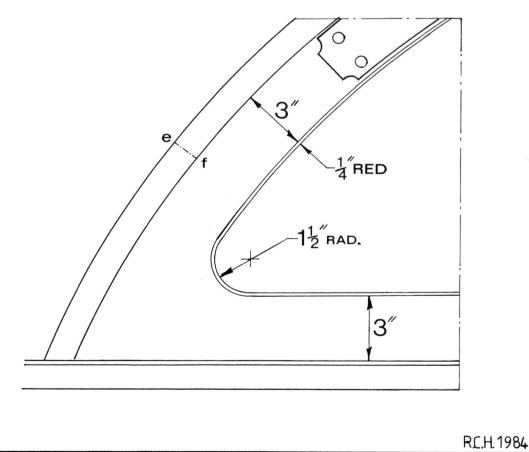

R.C.H. 1984

65

straight splashers on certain classes, such as the 'Experiments'. Soon the practice was altered, so that the lining continued straight to the end of the footplate edging, the change taking place perhaps about 1880. On the '17″ Coal Engines' and all subsequent classes, the dragbox was formed of a steel casting with rounded ends, shaped so as to merge into the footplate edging. The lining then continued round the end and vertically downwards across the end of the dragbox.

Openings cut in the angle to give access to coupling-rod ends, as on most passenger engines, were lined in the same way, with the grey line against the opening. This sometimes necessitated the red line being placed nearer to the grey, so as to fit all the lines into the space available.

Splashers

Splashers having tapered radial slots (that is, on certain pre-Webb designs) had the grey line on the periphery of the beading with the cream line inside it; the red line was on the splasher about $1\frac{1}{4}″$ from the cream. The slots themselves were lined in the same way as openings in footplate edging described above, with the grey line against the slot and the red about $\frac{1}{2}″$ outside the cream. On the plain splashers of Webb's and subsequent designs,

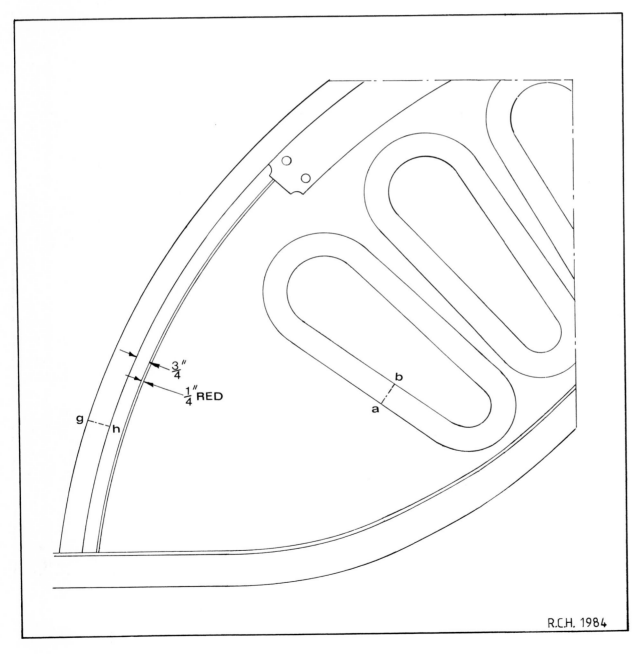

R.C.H. 1984

Figure 12 *(R.C.Hunt)*
Lining on slotted splashers. See (11b) page 64 for detail drawings of lining on the beading.

66

the grey and cream were on the beading as before but the $\frac{1}{4}''$ red line was also on the beading about $\frac{1}{4}''$ away from the cream. The beading was $4\frac{1}{2}''$ wide, though it measured $1\frac{5}{16}''$ on some of the later engines. In addition, there was another red line, $\frac{1}{4}''$ to $\frac{5}{16}''$ wide, forming a panel on the splasher, and normally placed $4\frac{1}{4}''$ from the periphery (that is, $3''$ from the bead) and $3''$ from the bottom edge. The radius of the bottom corners was $1\frac{1}{2}''$. Where the nameplate had a downward extension in the centre, the line followed its shape. Photographs of some engines, especially the 'Problems' with their large splashers, show this line about $\frac{1}{2}''$ further in.

On engines with straight-topped splashers, the same rules were generally observed. They were fully lined on the beading and had an inner red line forming a panel on the splasher proper. But there was one peculiarity on the 'Experiments', 'Prince of Wales' and '19" Goods'. On these engines the lines were curved down at the rear end to disappear completely where the splasher joined the panel. The coupling rod splasher was treated in the same way, the downward curve being placed directly under that on the main splasher above it, so that the lining ended short of the end of the beading, which because of the extra width and the curved corner of the cab panel was slightly longer.

The lining on the splashers of coal engines with $4'5\frac{1}{2}''$ wheels was similar, except that the red line on the beading was omitted and that on the splasher proper was $1''$ inside the beading and $1\frac{1}{4}''$ above the footplate. On the larger splashers of the '18 Goods', these dimensions were slightly larger, $1\frac{1}{16}''$ and $1\frac{3}{4}''$ on one engine measured. The small coupling rod splashers on the '18"' $0-6-2$Ts were similarly lined but not those on the 'Special DX', which were plain black.

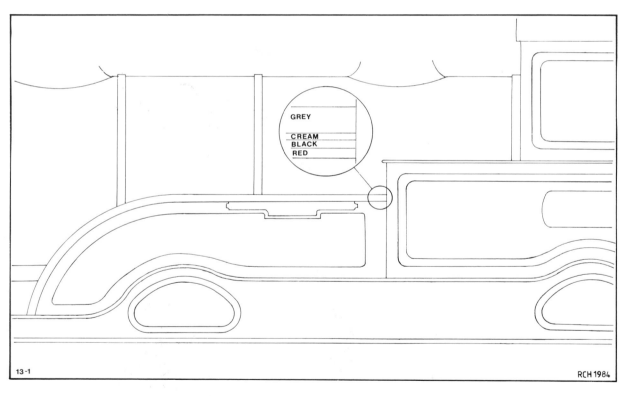

Figure 13 *(R.C.Hunt)*
Lining on straight-topped splashers: 1) as on 'Georges' and 'Claughtons' 2) as on 'Experiments', '19" Goods' and 'Prince of Wales'.

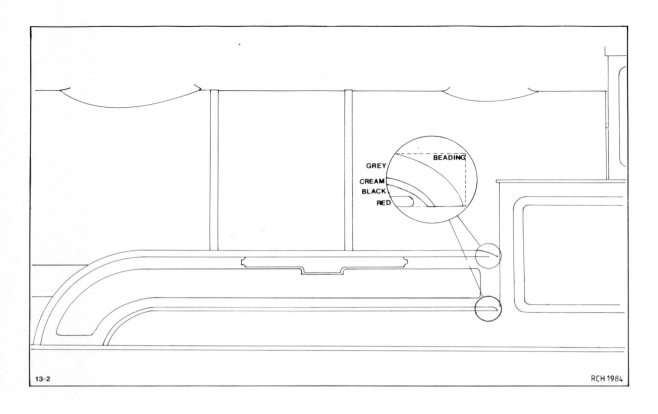

GREY
CREAM
BLACK
RED
BEADING

13-2   RCH 1984

Plate 77 *(E. Dutton collection)*
Broadside view of No. 1400, the
first 'Bill Bailey'. Despite the
straight splasher and the unusual contour of the footplating, the lining follows the
usual principles. As well as the
slide bars and connecting rod,
the coupling rods are now bright
too, since they are the fluted
type introduced in the mid
1890s, which were always
bright.

Ramsbottom engines and the earlier three-cylinder compounds had splashers over the leading wheels. They were lined in the same sort of way as those of goods engines but the lining was continued all round, on the inner edge as well as the outer, to form a panel. Photographs show that the position of the red line varied considerably and should be studied for any particular engine.

Some Variations from Standard

Ramsbottom passenger engines painted during the first year or so of the new livery had some additional lining. This comprised lining the bottom edge of the tender frame and the spring pads in the same style as the footplate edging. Some engines had the engine footsteps lined as well and a single red line round the tyres. These extra embellishments do not appear on all photographs of similar date, so it cannot be estimated how many engines actually received them. They are probably merely instances where the new livery had not been settled in its details. SHAH OF PERSIA, the earliest engine known to have received the lined black livery, had all these features and also had the tender footsteps lined. However, this engine might have been given a special finish for the occasion.

Another minor variation occurred with COLUMBINE and so presumably all Trevithick engines. Measurement of the lining in the 1930s showed the grey lines to be $\frac{5}{8}''$ wide in general, the cream $\frac{1}{8}''$ and the red $\frac{1}{4}''$. The splasher beading was only 1'' wide and the dimensions of the lining were: $\frac{1}{2}''$ grey, $\frac{1}{8}''$ cream, $\frac{3}{16}''$ space and $\frac{3}{16}''$ red.

Positioning of the Coat of Arms

Up to 1904 the coat of arms was always placed in the centre of the driving-wheel splasher but when straight-topped splashers appeared, the coat of arms was positioned so as to present the most symmetrical appearance. The 'Greater Britain' and 'John Hick' compounds, of course, had two splashers, each with a coat of arms, on either side; but as the drive was divided, both were in effect driving-wheel splashers.

The longitudinal positions of the coat of arms, and also of the nameplate where fitted, on engines with straight-topped splashers were as follows:
'Bill Bailey 4−6−0: over the centre coupled axle.
'Experiment', 'Prince of Wales' and '19″ Goods': midway between the first two coupled axles.
'George the Fifth' 4−4−0: midway between the driving axle and the rear of the splasher.
'Claughton' 4−6−0: approximately 1′ 7″ ahead of the centre coupled axle.

On the 'Precursor Tanks' the coat of arms was directly above the 'N' of 'L & N W R' on the tank sides and on the 4−6−2 tanks it was placed on the small cab side-sheet above the tank.

Bufferbeams

The front bufferbeams of all engines, and the rear bufferbeams of tank engines also, were painted red; the rear bufferbeams of tender engines were always black. The standard red bufferbeam had a black border, $\frac{3}{4}''$ wide, all round the edge, and a narrower black line, about $\frac{1}{2}''$, round the circular wooden pads on which the buffers were mounted, or round the bases of the buffers themselves in the later engines which did not have pads. Between the buffers was a black line, about $\frac{1}{4}''$ wide, forming a rectangular panel with rounded corners of $1\frac{1}{2}''$ radius. The panel was $10\frac{1}{2}''$ high on 15″ high bufferbeams, and 13″ high on 18″ beams. Its ends were located midway between the two lines of bolt heads inside each buffer, that is, opposite the centre lines of the main frames. Both the wooden pads and the buffers were black. The fully lined bufferbeam was applied to all engines even to those which were painted plain black, such as the unrebuilt 'DX' class. A number of photographs of 'Benbow' compounds, however, which seem to have been taken in the years before the grouping, appear to have completely unlined bufferbeams. These may have been due simply to wartime economies.

Figure 14 *(R.C.Hunt)*
Drawing of lining on 15″ high
bufferbeam.

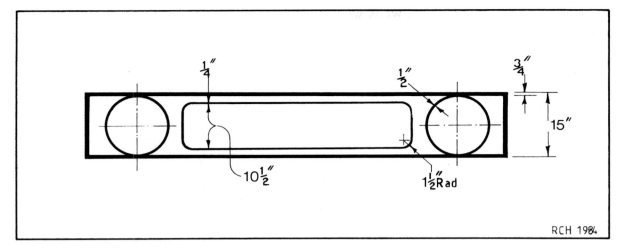

In one particularly clear photograph of the 'Greater Britain' class three-cylinder compound PRINCE GEORGE in obviously new paint there is an interesting variation on the standard scheme. The black border is on the face of the bufferbeam, with another $\frac{1}{2}$″ of red between it and the black ends and top edge. Other photographs do not provide such clear evidence but this feature seems to have been confined to certain three-cylinder compounds. An equally good photograph of the Whale 'Precursor' ACHILLES shows that there was no such red edging and that the bufferbeam was painted completely according to the standard scheme. Another variation is seen in F.Moore's paintings of the four-cylinder compound $4-4-0$s, which have a red band round the buffer sockets. However, this does not show up in any photograph, with the possible exception of one of CORN-WALL, and it would be expected to be apparent on official Crewe photographs, on which, though the engines are in a special photographic finish, the lining is always accurate.

Cab interiors

Precise details of the colour of paints used for the inside of engine cabs (side panels, spectacle plate and roof) are extremely difficult to establish. The few published sources vary considerably but a consensus seems to be some sort of reddish-brown. The earliest record is in *The English Mechanic* for 24th October 1890: 'colour inside cab dullish red'; but *The Locomotive Magazine*, February 1896, gives 'light brown'. Other sources give red brown, dirty putty and grained oak.

Certainly, however, the majority of cabs from Webb's time onwards were painted what was officially termed 'indian red'. In fact, this was indian red (more correctly, red oxide of iron tempered with ivory black), and so was a dullish shade; it can be accurately represented on models by mixing two parts of indian red with one part of ivory black.

It is suggested that some engines, such as certain 'George the Fifths', had cabs painted dirty putty some time before the First World War, Bowen Cooke being responsible for the change. Whatever the truth may be, many Cooke engines had indian red cabs. Colonel Cantlie clearly remembers the interior of a 'Claughton' cab in its pre-war livery as being 'reddish buff', with the names of the two drivers painted (presumably, in black) on the left-hand side-sheet above the driver's head. Each main-line engine had two drivers to facilitate the administration of the coal bonus scheme introduced early in the Cooke period.

A grained oak finish was introduced, probably only in late 1921 when lining was resumed, but even then most engines are believed to still have had cabs painted indian red, even those which were fully lined at that time. Indeed, a careful observer, who was noting livery details at this period, recorded no other colour on any engine.

Frames

The frames were painted black both inside and out. Motion plates, when built up from sheet and angle, were black also, but when cast-steel plates were introduced, they were

71

painted vermilion. The crank webs were painted white at one time but later the motion generally, including the crank webs, was machined bright. In service it had a thin film of oil overall, the numbers stamped on the parts being clearly visible. The change was made to enable any flaws or cracks in the metal to be clearly seen. It is believed to have occurred in the 1890s, perhaps when fluted coupling rods, which were always unpainted, were introduced.

In an article in the *SLS Journal*, Vol 11, W.J.Reynolds, who was well acquainted with the Webb compounds by personal observation, states that the inside of their main frames was painted reddish brown (presumably indian red). This seems to be contradicted, however, by a letter from W.Nowell Davies, who was a Crewe pupil from 1901 to 1910 and who also knew the Webb compounds well, to J.M.Dunn. He states that the first ten 'Precursors', built in 1904, had the inside of their frames painted vermilion as an experiment, that the experiment was unsuccessful and that black paint was resumed. This at least implies that black paint was general before the experiment and was continued afterwards.

Brightwork

In photographs various parts can be seen finished bright. In the earlier days these seem to vary with the individual tastes of the enginemen. Brass parts, such as lubricators, cab spectacle frames, whistle and reducing valve were invariably polished and in the Webb period many chimney caps were burnished, along with cylinder covers on compounds, hand rails, smokebox door wheels, buffers, front couplings and so on. Connecting rods were always bright, as were fluted coupling rods from their introduction in 1897.

An instruction issued by Bowen Cooke to cleaners in 1908 clearly specified which parts were to be polished bright: 'hand rails, angle iron round tank tops, hand pillars [that is, vertical hand rails on cabs], coupling rods, spindle rods and weigh bars'. They were 'to be greased over with cleaning oil then scoured over with No. 1 emery or bath brick and oil, and a little tallow rubbed over them'. Nevertheless, at this period too, certain engines had additional embellishments, no doubt as the result of the individual tastes of their crews. SIR GILBERT CLAUGHTON had a burnished chimney cap for a time when new and so did other 'Claughtons'; and many 'Princes' about 1920 had buffers, front coupling, smokebox door wheel and other parts beautifully polished. The best guide to a particular class at a particular period is the study of a number of photographs.

Lettering

Unlike many railway companies, the LNWR generally felt no need to advertise the ownership of its locomotives by putting its initials on them. Indeed many engines displayed no outward indication of ownership whatsoever, other than their distinctive livery and appearance. However, three classes of tank engines introduced in the twentieth century carried the company's initials on the tank sides as a matter of course. Whale's 'Precursor

Figure 15 *(Alan Gettings)*
Lettering as applied to 'Precursor Tanks'.

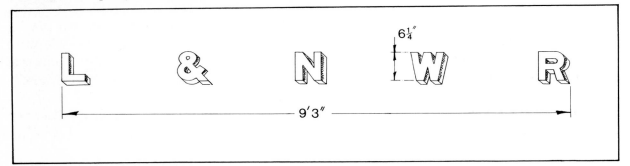

Tanks' had 'L & N W R' in gold letters 6¼" high (the manufacturer's description was 'Genuine Gold Leaf'); Bowen Cooke's 4−6−2 tanks had 'L N W R' in yellow ochre

letters 12″ high; and his 0 – 8 – 2 shunting tanks had 'L N W R' in yellow ochre letters 9½″ high. All these were block letters and were shaded in red below and to the right.

Photographs exist of two of the 4 – 6 – 2 tanks with much larger letters but these were for trial and photographic purposes only. In traffic they carried the normal 12″ letters. In later years some of the 4 – 6 – 2 tanks received 9½″ letters like the 0 – 8 – 2 tanks, and 9½″ letters of LNWR style were also used to display 'L M S' on the first of Beames 0 – 8 – 4 tanks and on some 4 – 6 – 2 tanks in the early post-grouping period.

The only engine to carry the letters 'L N W R' on its tender was the 'George the Fifth' class 4 – 4 – 0 No. 956 DACHSHUND, which carried them for about six months in 1911 purely as an experiment. The letters are believed to have been 9½″ high, as used on the 0 – 8 – 2 tanks.

Numberplates, Tender Numberplates, Shed Plates

The numberplates introduced early in 1873 were made of cast iron. Above the number was the legend 'L & N W R' and below it 'CREWE WORKS'. The number and the border of the numberplate were painted yellow but the subsidiary legends were always painted vermilion along with the background. In 1877, starting with No. 890 SIR HARDMAN EARLE, the first of the second batch of 'Precedents', numberplates were cast in brass, with all numerals, border and subsidiary legends polished. Cast-iron numberplates with painted numerals and border, as before, continued to be used for duplicate-list engines.

In 1906 this style of plate was superseded by a new one incorporating the date when the engine was built, the month and year, and omitting the company's initials. The earlier plates were all of the same size but the new plates varied according to the number of digits in the number. As before, the new plates were of brass, with all characters and border polished and with a vermilion background. The first engines to have the new type were the 'Precursor Tanks', introduced in May 1906, but the last engines to have the old style of plate were some, if not all, of the batch of 'Experiments' built in September-December of that year.

During the First World War, in 1915 it is believed, numberplates were again made of cast iron, as an economy measure. At about the same time the numbers '6' and '9' were interchanged, the former becoming an upside down version of the latter, and *vice versa*. This seems to have come about merely by mistake but it had a decidedly detrimental effect on the appearance. At some stage after the war brass numberplates are thought to have been produced again, but whether this applied to all plates or just a few is not known.

73

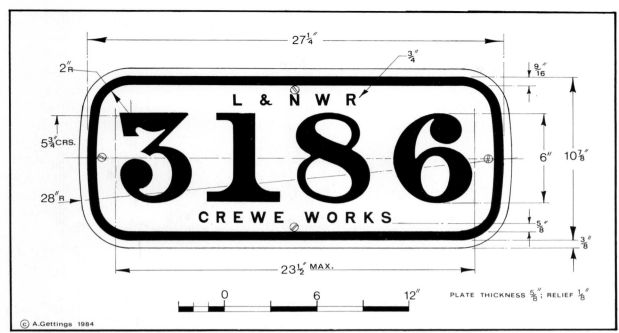

Figure 16 *(Alan Gettings)*
Drawing of typical Webb numberplate.

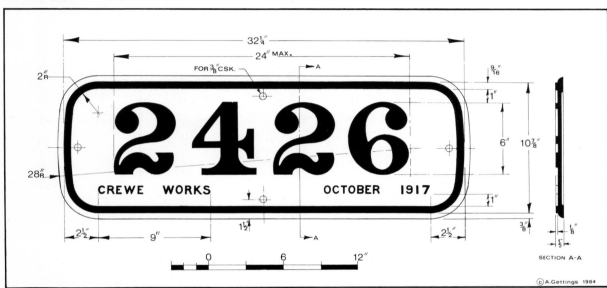

Figure 17 *(Alan Gettings)*
Drawing of typical Whale numberplate.

Figure 18 *(Alan Gettings)*
Numerals used on numberplates. The numerals painted on bufferbeams and cabsides before Webb introduced plates, were in the same style but shaded.

The preserved 'Jumbo' HARDWICKE, whose numberplates were presumably made by the LMS, appears to have cast-iron plates with the post-1915 '9'.

Tenders were numbered in the same way as engines, that is, when a tender was scrapped, its number was transferred to its replacement. There was no relationship between engine and tender numbers, both being numbered in completely separate series. A tender number was carried on a small cast-iron plate bolted to the back plate of the tank. The border and the characters were picked out in white in many cases but equally often the whole plate was painted black.

The shed number was displayed on a small oval plate, $5'' \times 3\frac{1}{2}''$; it was of white enamel and had black figures $2''$ high. The plate was carried in a holder fixed to the angle iron at the rear of the cab roof. When this type of plate was introduced is not known but it was certainly in use in 1878. *The English Mechanic* for 26th July records: 'Shed plate — oval-shaped white enamel tab, black figures on it'.

Figure 19a *(Alan Gettings)*
A typical tender numberplate.

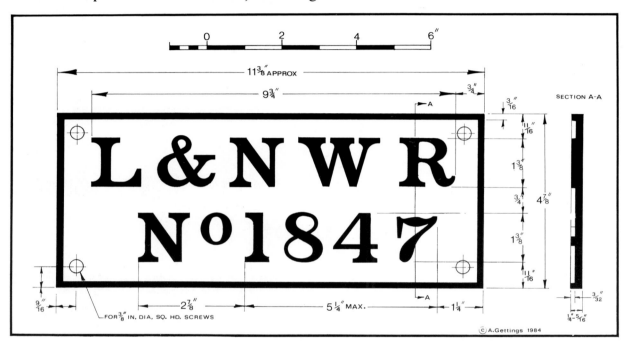

Figure 19b *(Alan Gettings)*
Numerals used on tender numberplates.

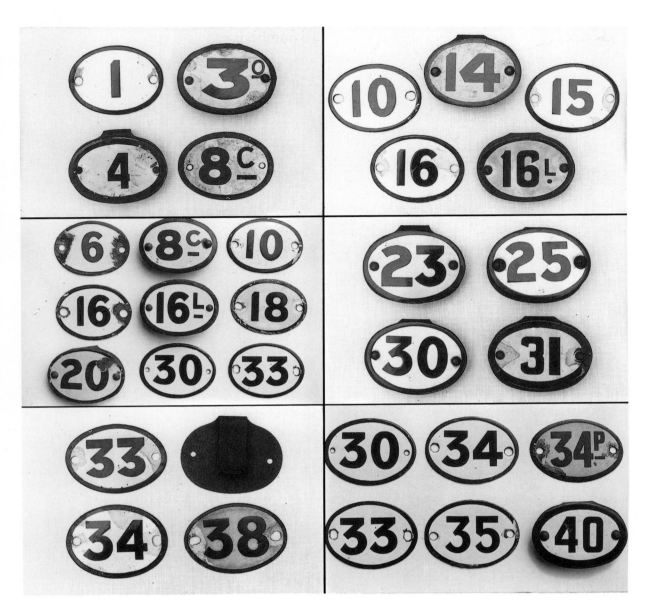

Plate 80   *(E. Talbot)*
A selection of shed plates.
Those with numerals in a later
more angular style were made in
LMS days.

Nameplates

The well known LNWR style of nameplate originated in the very early days of Crewe Works if not before. In its typical form the letters of the name were cut into a strip of brass, filled with black engine stopping and painted over with black japan paint, at least in the later days. In Ramsbottom's time the letters are believed to have been chrome green in colour, similar to the engines.

The earliest type of plate showed only the name. Known examples of this kind of plate were made in 1847 (CORNWALL) and in 1859 (the 'Problem' WATT). At some stage a type of plate was in use, which showed in addition to the name the legend 'CREWE WORKS' on the left and the date the engine was built on the right. Plates of this kind can be seen in a number of photographs of Trevithick singles. Both these types of plates cannot be dated precisely but by August 1861 the typical curved plate had been adopted. This carried the legends 'CREWE WORKS', 'L & N W R Cº' and the building date in two rows on either side of the name. Plates of this kind were last made, with the exception of a few replacements, for Whale's 'Precursors'. The brass strip was $2\frac{3}{4}''$ wide, the letters making up the name were $2\frac{1}{4}''$ high and the smaller letters $\frac{5}{8}''$ high. A smaller straight version of this plate was produced for the 18in-gauge Crewe Works shunters, with letters $1\frac{3}{8}''$ high; and another variation occurred with the plates of the first batch of 'Experi-

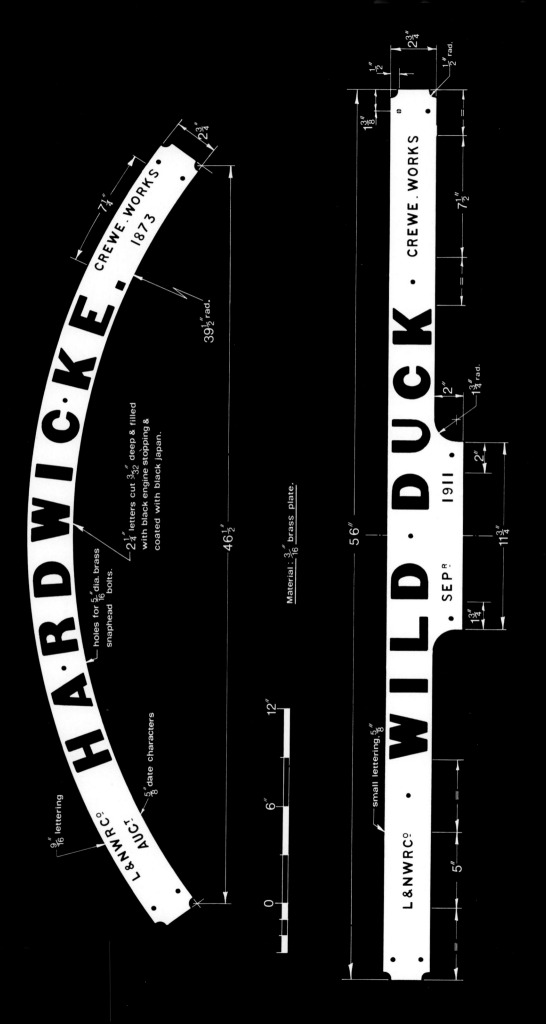

H·A·R·D·W·I·C·K·E·

CREWE·WORKS 1873

L&NWRCº AUGT

7¼″

2¾″
2¾″

39½″ rad.

46½″

holes for ⁵⁄₁₆″ dia. brass snaphead bolts.

2¼″ letters cut ³⁄₃₂″ deep & filled with black engine stopping & coated with black japan.

⁹⁄₁₆″ lettering

⁵⁄₈″ date characters

Material : ³⁄₁₆″ brass plate.

0   6″   12″

W·I·L·D· ·D·U·C·K·

CREWE· WORKS

L&NWRCº · SEPR 1911 ·

small lettering, ⁵⁄₈″

2¾″

½″

½″ rad.

1⅛″

7½″

2″

1¾″ rad.

2″

11¾″

1¾″

56″

5″

2″

½″

Figure 20   *(Alan Gettings)*
Typical curved and straight nameplates.

ment' compounds, which had plates with a wider centre portion carrying the inscription 'F.W.WEBB'S PATENT', replaced by 'F.W.WEBB'S SYSTEM' with the 1884 batch. The 2 − 2 − 2 − 2 compounds had two plates on either side and the minor inscriptions were re-distributed.

Named engines after the 'Precursors' all had straight nameplates. The basic dimensions remained the same but the widened centre portion of the compounds was used and the minor inscriptions were again re-distributed. In Ramsbottom's time plates varied in length according to the name but early in the Webb period standard lengths were introduced for each class. 'Claughton' plates, for instance, were usually 6′ long. However, there were numerous exceptions, especially, but not always, where names were too long to fit on the standard length.

Most plates which differed from the two standard types of curved and straight plates did so in very minor ways indeed. For instance, a few 'Claughtons' and 'Princes' named after the grouping had 'L M S' inscribed on their plates instead of 'L & N W R Cº', though the plates were otherwise perfectly standard. The only major exception occurred in the case of the War Memorial 'Claughton' No. 1914 PATRIOT, whose plates were basically in the standard style but were enlarged to carry beneath the name the words: 'In memory of the fallen L&NWR employees 1914-1919'.

During the Webb era cast plates were introduced for use on departmental engines, not so much to act as nameplates but to denote the allocation of the engine. Exceptions were EUSTON and LIVERPOOL, though here again those engines were probably originally intended to work at the place whose names they carried. These plates were generally made of brass and like numberplates were polished with vermilion backgrounds.

The one major example of a non-standard cast plate was that produced for 'George the Fifth' No. 5000 CORONATION. This was special in every respect, with letters of unusual design, a crown above the name and the following legend beneath it: '5000th engine built at the locomotive works Crewe June 1911'; the background was painted vermilion.

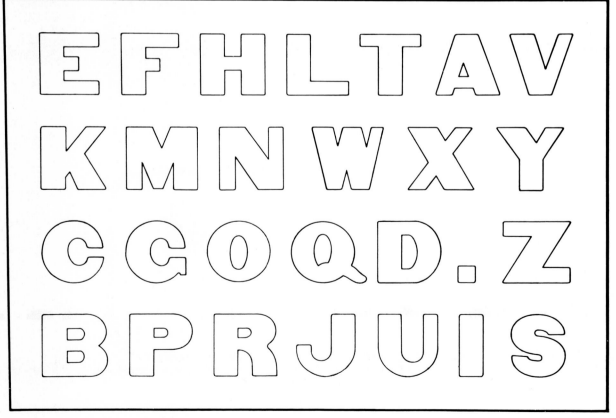

Figure 21 *(Alan Gettings)*
Alphabet used for nameplates.

Plate 81
A selection of preserved name-plates, along with a number-plate (with the post-1915 '6'), a tender numberplate (with the later style of numeral) and a shed plate.

Figure 23 *(Alan Gettings)*
Drawings of ENGINEER WALSALL and HOLYHEAD (DNGR).

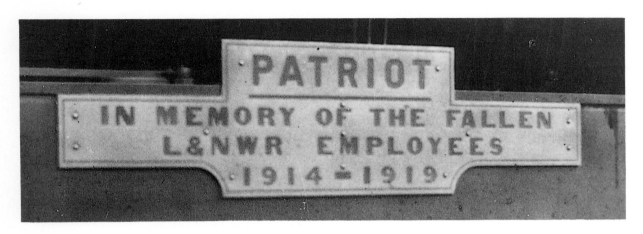

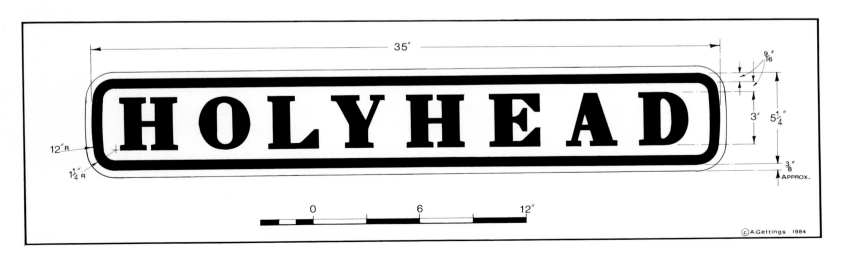

Plate 85 *(L.Hanson)*
The unique design of nameplate
fitted to CORONATION.

Specially Finished Locomotives

At various times certain engines were given special finishes in honour of particular events.

SHAH OF PERSIA

Apart from its temporary nameplate in arabic characters and a large crown between dome and chimney, 'Problem' No. 806 only had some additional lining, as previously described, in honour of the visit of the Shah to Crewe Works in 1873. The extra lining was probably no more than a trial of the new livery.

GREATER BRITAIN, QUEEN EMPRESS

In honour of the Diamond Jubilee of Queen Victoria two of F.W.Webb's 'Greater Britain' class three-cylinder compounds, GREATER BRITAIN and QUEEN EMPRESS, were taken into Crewe Works in about May 1897 and given special and costly liveries of red and white respectively. These engines were probably the most magnificently finished locomotives ever to run in this country or indeed anywhere on earth. Contemporary descriptions of them differ slightly in their details, but so far as can be ascertained, the following account is accurate.

On No. 2053 GREATER BRITAIN, the boiler and cylinder cleadings, cab, splashers, footplate edging and tender tank were painted scarlet and lined out with gold leaf 1″ wide, edged with dark blue, $\frac{1}{2}$″ wide on the outside and $\frac{1}{8}$″ wide on the inside. Inside this again was a second gold line, $\frac{1}{2}$″ wide, edged with $\frac{1}{4}$″ and $\frac{1}{16}$″ dark blue on the outside and inside respectively. These lines were placed similarly to those on a normal black engine. The boiler cleading bands were edged with polished brass on the outer edge of which was a dark blue line; the bands themselves seem to have been dark blue between the brass, though this is not mentioned in the account. Smokebox, frames and wheels were dark blue, and the tyres were white, while the front bufferbeam was lined out in gold, where normally there would be black. The leading splashers and the tender were adorned with the LNWR coat of arms and the trailing splashers had the Royal Arms. As usual, the numberplate was of polished brass but with a dark blue background.

No. 2054 QUEEN EMPRESS was painted creamy white (probably white with a slight cream effect due to the varnish) where GREATER BRITAIN was scarlet. The lining was

81

the same as on GREATER BRITAIN but the edges of the panels, together with the smokebox, frames above footplate level, sandboxes and footplate edging were of a colour described in different accounts as light grey, blue, mauve and lilac. Another difference was that the front of the cab was lined — unique on the LNWR. The wheels, tyres and front bufferbeam were as on GREATER BRITAIN, and the same coats of arms were carried on the splashers. In the middle of the sides of the tender were brass plates the size of numberplates, which were engraved with thick and thin lines filled with black engine stopping like nameplates, to depict side views of locomotives; they showed the first engine built at Wolverton in 1845, the Bury 2 – 2 – 0 No. 92, and QUEEN EMPRESS as it was in 1897.

QUEEN EMPRESS was repainted in the standard black livery in about October 1897 and GREATER BRITAIN about July 1898, though both engines retained the brass boiler bands for some time.

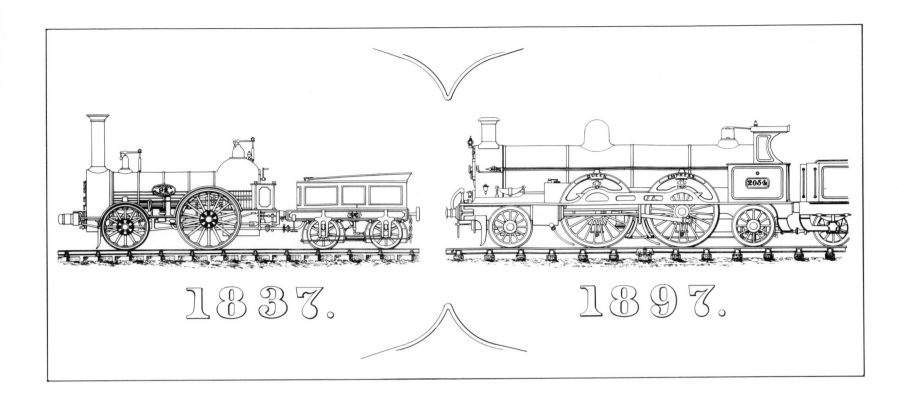

GLADSTONE

For working the funeral train of William Ewart Gladstone on 25th May 1898, 'Precedent' No. 1521 GLADSTONE was painted with grey bands in place of the usual red, cream
and grey, and the bufferbeam was also painted grey. GLADSTONE worked the train
between Broughton Hall (Flint) and Willesden Junction. The train was taken on to
Westminster Bridge (Metropolitan District Railway) for the funeral service in Westminster
Abbey by 4'6" 2−4−2 tank No. 788, but it is not known if this engine was similarly
painted.

CORONATION

The introduction of Bowen Cooke's superheated development of the 'Precursors' in 1909 coincided with the accession of King George V and accordingly the new engine was named after the new monarch. In the following year the coronation ceremony coincided with the completion of another of the class bearing Crewe motion No. 5000 and the two events were celebrated by giving the engine a special finish. However, the scheme was not so grand as those of the Webb engines in 1897, being no more than an elaboration of the standard black livery. The boiler cleading bands were edged with brass, the wheel bosses and tyres were polished bright and the Royal Arms were carried in the centre of the tender side. Perhaps the most striking feature was the nameplate, which had raised letters on a vermilion ground, surmounted by a crown.

Plate 88 *(E.Dutton collection)*
No. 5000 CORONATION in its special livery.

PATRIOT

Early in 1920 a new batch of 'Claughtons' was built, incorporating a number of improvements, and it was decided to make the first one into the company's war memorial engine. At first the number was to be 69, which was the next number available in the LNWR numbering system, but this was changed during construction to 1914, a much more appropriate choice. Standard cast-iron numberplates with vermilion backgrounds were fitted at first but when the engine was brought out for inspection and photography, the CME thought them too bright for a war memorial engine and had them replaced by brass ones with black backgrounds. The engine was named PATRIOT and was painted in plain dull black, with no lining and no coat of arms. The nameplate was of special design and was unique, since at least the 1860s, in making no mention of Crewe Works or the date of building.

(E.Dutton collection)
Interior view of clerestory dining saloon built in the late 1890s.

6

COACHING STOCK

by **Philip Millard**

Constituent Companies

The constituent companies varied greatly in the quality of the passenger accommodation they provided, and uniformity in facilities was neither attempted nor conceived. The Liverpool & Manchester, Grand Junction and London & Birmingham Railways operated mail coaches, a superior first class, which were painted in imitation of the Royal Mail coaches used on the roads. Some railways provided only first- and second-class carriages, and did not introduce third class until compelled to do so by the Act of 1844. On some companies all carriages were painted in the same colour scheme, but on others different colours were used to denote the different classes. Through running, however, was in operation quite early; carriages ran through from Lancaster to Euston, for example, from the opening of the Lancaster & Preston Junction Railway in 1840.

Details of the liveries of the early companies have been gathered mainly from contemporary accounts.

Bolton & Leigh Railway 1828-1845

First-class coaches were green, both the bodies and the wheels, and displayed the company's coat of arms on panels. Two coaches were named, ELEPHANT and CASTLE, after the main features of the coat of arms of the town of Bolton.

Liverpool & Manchester Railway 1830-1845

The mail coaches were red with black upper panels, while first-class coaches were yellow, again with black upper panels, and were named, for example, GREYHOUND, DESPATCH and TRAVELLER, in imitation of road coaches. Second-class carriages were blue and, at first, were open, but from October 1844 open carriages were designated third class and the seconds were enclosed.

North Union Railway 1831-1845

First-class coaches were green picked out with black. A model in the National Railway Museum is green with black uppers and displays the Preston coat of arms on the body, the lamb and flag.

Grand Junction Railway 1837-1846

Mail coaches were red (probably scarlet) with black upper panels. First-class coaches were chocolate with black upper panels. They bore names, such as TRIUMPH, SWALLOW, STATESMAN and HIBERNIA, and were lettered 'GRAND JUNCTION

RAILWAY' round the bottom of the centre compartment. The colour of the seconds is not known but at least some had black upper panels. They were not named but were lettered 'GRAND JUNCTION RAILWAY' along the waist in a straight line. Third-class coaches were introduced in 1839 and were open but no details of their livery are known.

London & Birmingham Railway 1837-1846

Mail coaches were red with black upper panels. A board minute of 1837 specifies: the 'colour and decorations to be as near as possible to the Royal Mails now in use'. First-class coaches were green with black upper panels, while the seconds were perhaps also green and had lettering in gold, relieved with dark green. The open excursion stock, which was in use at the start and was discontinued by October 1837, was also green; and the third-class coaches, which were introduced in 1840 and were open, were perhaps green too. Carriage trucks were green picked out with black.

One of the mail coaches was converted for the use of Queen Adelaide, the dowager queen of King William IV, in October 1839. In all probability this is the vehicle now on display at the National Railway Museum, despite the fact that the date 1842 is usually quoted for it. It is now claret with black upper panels, lined gold and red, and carries the L&BR coat of arms and the 'L&BR' monogram in italic script.

Another coach was ordered for Queen Victoria in September 1842, and was described and illustrated in the *Illustrated London News*, 2nd December 1843: 'dark lake (the Queen's colour) relieved with scarlet and gold, the upper quarterings having a broad border of French white round the plate glass windows in either panel'. The engraving is probably the source of the mistaken belief that white upper panels dated from the very beginning of the LNWR.

It was possibly the influence of these vehicles, or the through working of GJR carriages, that led to the change from green to lake on first-class carriages at some stage, either on the L&BR or on the LNWR Southern Division.

Lancaster & Preston Junction Railway 1840-1849

When they were sold in 1849, all carriages, first, second and third class, were green. Some vehicles were yellow at first and had names, but possibly the account refers to Liverpool & Manchester stock on loan or working through.

Manchester & Birmingham Railway 1842-1846

First-class coaches were painted dark blue.

The first twenty-five years

After the amalgamation of 1846, separate carriage departments were at first retained for the Northern and Southern Divisions, at Crewe and Saltley. In the 1850s the respective carriage superintendents were Mr Worsdell and Mr Slater. Both works built carriages to their own separate and varied designs and it was not until 1860, when Richard Bore became carriage superintendent at Saltley, that standardisation began. Shortly before that, construction had ceased at Crewe, which then became responsible only for maintenance, and in 1865 the carriage works was moved to Wolverton and Saltley was closed.

In view of the diversity of design practice between Saltley and Crewe, the two superintendents probably took an independent attitude to colour schemes as well, though at this distance in time only fragmentary details survive. One of the plates in Fare's *Con-*

trasts, published in 1852, shows an LNWR passenger luggage van painted brown with a black top, while the cover of a music-hall song entitled *The Railway Guard* and published about the same time shows a bearded guard wearing the bandolier of the LNWR across his chest and standing in front of second-class carriage No. 139, which is green. Following the introduction of varnished teak carriages on the Great Northern Railway, the LNWR experimented with this finish in 1851 but ultimately decided not to adopt it. During the mid-1850s first-class carriages seem to have had lake or dark claret lower panels while the upper panels were painted black, a practice inherited from the constituent companies and which was common in both road and railway carriages of the time. Both second- and third-class carriages were green, and it is clear from the minutes that in 1858 'Quaker green' paint was being regularly purchased.

A number of clues are to be found in the minutes of the stores committee from 1857 onwards. In December of that year, Mr Slater, of Saltley, recommended 'light upper panels as the black was so easily injured by the sun's heat'. Early in the following year, specimen paint schemes were prepared for the directors, one having cream upper panels picked out in claret. The cream was evidently not adopted, for in July 1858 it was decided to recommend that the upper panels of firsts continued to be painted 'drab colour' for a while, the lower panels being lake. At the same meeting the carriage superintendents were instructed to consider whether some other colour could not be introduced in place of lake. On 11th November 1858 the committee 'inspected a number of carriages painted by Messrs Worsdell and Slater, and decided that the colours be lake and drab sides, with brown ends'. No class is mentioned but subsequent minutes make it clear that by this time first- and second-class carriages were lake, and third-class green, all with 'drab' upper panels. Thus, it would appear that second-class carriages changed from green to lake in 1858, possibly as a result of the introduction of first- and second-class composite carriages. A minute of November 1859 called for 'FIRST' and 'SECOND' to be printed on the doors of composites, which perhaps implies that carriages of a particular class were previously recognisable by their colour.

At this period most trains conveyed only first- and second-class passengers, third-class being catered for only by the cheap 'Parliamentary' trains, which stopped at all stations and which were generally provided only once a day. Naturally, third-class carriages were painted in a much simpler style and were doubtless devoid of any elaborate decoration.

In July 1859 Messrs Slater and Worsdell were instructed to agree on one shade of green and one shade of lake to be worked to in future. In the following month sample boards were submitted to the stores committee showing the proposed future painting of first- and second-class carriages. The Saltley sample of lake was chosen, and this was signed by the chairman and 'ordered to be kept in a dark place' to prevent the colour fading. No sample of green appears to have been considered, nor was any reference to the colour of the upper panels made.

In July 1861 Mr Bore reported that 'in the train prepared for the Rainhill traffic he had painted the third-class carriages brown and drab, instead of green and drab, and wished to know whether the committee would like the alteration to be made in the colour of the third-class stock as they came into the shops for repainting'. The matter was referred to the traffic committee, which decided against the change.

In June 1862, when the formation of the West Coast Joint Stock was being discussed, it was specified that the new carriages (which were actually built in November 1862 though they did not enter service until the following March) should be painted with white upper panels and 'dark claret' lower panels, and should carry a heraldic shield bearing a lion rampant, with the words 'WEST COAST JOINT STOCK' on a ribbon. Two of the new carriages were third class, but no mention of any different colour scheme was made.

In January 1869 the locomotive committee ordered that first, second and composite carriages were 'to be painted the dark claret colour with white upper panels, the same as the West Coast Joint Stock', while 'the thirds were to remain green as at present'. It was specified that the lettering on the doors should be confined to the words 'FIRST',

'SECOND' or 'THIRD'. Mr Bore suggested that for the sake of uniformity the horse boxes and carriage trucks should be painted the same colour as the carriages, but the committee resolved that no alteration be made. Nearly three years later, in December 1871, it was decided to paint the thirds and horseboxes maroon, 'the same as the other coaching stock', although some old third-class carriages were still green in May 1874.

Clearly, the terms 'claret', 'lake' and 'maroon' were all used at various times to describe the same colour, although 'lake' appears to be the correct official description.

From the evidence of the official minutes, therefore, the well known LNWR carriage livery would appear to date from 1869, or from 1863 as far as the WCJS is concerned. Nevertheless, photographs exist, known to have been taken before this date, which show white, or very light-coloured, upper panels. Examples are the Kirkburton train (*LNWR Miscellany, Volume 2,* Plate 187) of 1867, the view of Sutton Coldfield (*ibid, Plate 70*) taken in 1863 and one of Birmingham New Street published in the *Railway Magazine* for February 1952 said to be taken 'soon after it was opened' (1852-4) which would appear to be earlier still. Even the last vehicle in the Sutton Coldfield train, of much earlier date than the newly built stock to which it is attached, has white upper panels. A painting in the Science Museum of the Abergele accident of August 1868 shows all carriages in brown and off-white, not very different, if at all, from the later 'flake white' colour.

It would be interesting to know just what colour was meant by 'drab' and whether it was light enough to be confused with the white of later years on these old photographs. The term gives the impression of a dark buff or tan colour, but no photograph is known which shows anything that could be so interpreted. It has been suggested that in the last century 'drab' was used to describe the colour of natural unbleached wool, which would go some way to reconciling the various pieces of evidence. On the other hand, a contemporary dictionary quotes drab as being 'a dun colour, inclined to reddish-brown'.

The photographic evidence points to the conclusion that the familiar LNWR livery was adopted in 1859, or at the latest in 1862 at the time of the establishment of the West Coast Joint Stock, and that the minute of 1869 merely restates the position, perhaps emphasising that the third-class carriages should remain green and not be painted in the same manner as carriages of superior class. Even this raises difficulties, however, as both the Kirkburton and Sutton Coldfield trains include carriages which are clearly lettered 'THIRD CLASS', and the Sutton train at least is in lake.

Roofs at this time show the same variation between white and various shades of grey that is apparent in later days, with perhaps a predominance of the former. In default of further information, it seems reasonable to assume that they were turned out white from the works and are seen in traffic with varying thicknesses of grime.

There is no evidence as to whether carriages were lined out at this time. Mouldings were picked out in the body colour, with the possible exception of the bolection mouldings, that is, those surrounding the quarter lights, which like the droplight frames were in some cases, if not all, of varnished wood.

Lettering was located at waist level. In the Kirkburton branch train the leading vehicle has 'THIRD CLASS' between the two end doors in about 3″ shaded block letters, the initial 'T' and 'C' being 1″ larger, whilst the number (41?) is carried at the same level in the centre of the carriage in 3″ figures. The second coach in this train is a first/second composite and in this case the class designations are carried on the waist panels of the doors in smaller letters with the number rendered twice between each end pair of doors, much as in later practice. The Sutton Coldfield photograph shows a 'coupled train', 'set' in modern parlance, of suburban stock. The leading carriage is a brake third lettered 'L&NWR — THIRD-CLASS — 105' between the doors in approximately $2\frac{1}{2}$″ shaded characters, the initial 'T' and 'C' being larger, about $3\frac{1}{2}$″, whilst on the left-hand door of the double pair the word 'GUARD' appears in smaller letters, some $1\frac{1}{2}$-$1\frac{3}{4}$″ high. In photographs of this period there is no evidence of the company's coat of arms or monogram being displayed.

Before 1869 the numbers of WCJS carriages were displayed only on the inside of the

89

compartment doors, but in March of that year they were ordered 'to be painted on the panels also of each carriage to enable passengers to regain their seats more easily than is now practicable'.

The standard carriage livery

Whatever the exact date of its introduction, the carriage livery from 1872 at the very latest remained essentially unchanged until the grouping. The upper panels of the vehicles (including brake, luggage, parcels and similar vans constructed with passenger-style panels and mouldings) were 'flake white', which was obtained by mixing one pound of ultramarine blue with one hundredweight of white lead. When varnished with 'best pale finishing body varnish', this colour had a slightly greenish tinge which gradually disappeared as the varnish wore thin with repeated cleaning. The lower panels and all raised mouldings above the waist were painted alazarine carmine lake, or 'dark claret' as it was called in earlier days. The colour was also sometimes referred to as 'chocolate', although a Wolverton painting specification published in the *Railway Magazine* for November 1897 makes it clear that 'chocolate' and 'lake' are synonymous. Lining was applied to both edges of all mouldings (not the panels) both above and below the waist, and consisted of a $\frac{1}{2}''$ or $\frac{5}{8}''$ yellow line edged with a $\frac{1}{8}''$ white line. The yellow was a deep shade, which was intended to imitate gold, and was mixed from yellow ochre, lemon chrome and orange chrome pigments in the proportions of 5:3:1. It is possible that before about 1900 the lining was actually executed in gold leaf, at any rate on saloons and other vehicles intended for main-

Plate 89   *(G.H.Platt collection)*

First-class carriage No. 177, built in 1872, at Holyhead in 1880. Dimensions were 27′6″ long, 7′9″ wide and 7′2″ high. Some 103 vehicles to this design with three first-class compartments and a luggage cupboard were constructed between 1872 and 1875. According to the official records all but one were altered to four-compartment composites (mostly two first and two seconds, or two firsts and two thirds) in 1887-92, but no photographs of them in this condition have been discovered. Some were reduced to four wheels and the majority were supplemented between 1892 and 1899, withdrawal being in the 1905-10 period.

The coat of arms is carried on the door of the centre compartment and the monogram on those of the outer ones. The waist panel of the right-hand luggage door carries the word 'LUGGAGE', a practice which probably continued until the introduction of slate waist panels in 1886.

On the right is 30′ by 7′9″ luggage tri-composite No. 1256, one of about 130 constructed in 1872-3. In this case the coat of arms appears on the inner compartment doors (first and second class) and the monogram on the outer (third class) ones. On this vehicle the ventilator bonnets appear to be white rather than lake with a gold (later yellow) line along the lower edge of each ridge. Between 1885 and 1895 many of these carriages were re-classified as firsts or rebuilt as end-brake thirds; they were supplemented in 1892-9 and withdrawn between 1903 and 1914.

line use. Two $\frac{1}{8}''$ white lines (one only after 1916) were applied along the bottom of the carriage body, and there was a similar vertical white line at the extreme end, but these vertical white lines were never placed on, or immediately adjacent to, a guard's ogee. Ventilator bonnets were also lake and lined yellow and white on the bottom edge of each louvre. There was no lining around the door openings but the doors themselves had a $\frac{1}{8}''$ white line along the top edge and on both sides down to waist level only.

The ends of the carriage were painted lake in exactly the same manner as the sides, but without any lining. There is some evidence that the ends were at one time painted a dark brown colour, but several retired paint-shop employees at Wolverton, whose memory extends back to before the First World War, insist that the ends of the body were treated in exactly the same way as the sides. Since any change would almost certainly have been from lake ends to brown ends and not *vice versa* (as lake was considerably more expensive), and since the application of brown and lake called for different grades of painter, the recollections of contemporary employees can be accepted with confidence. The reference to brown probably refers to the gangway end boards of corridor carriages, although they seem to have changed to black during the first war. Certainly, those who remember carriages in LNWR livery cannot recall any difference between sides and ends, and none is visible in photographs.

Plate 90   *National Railway Museum (Crown Copyright)*
One of the pioneer radial carriages, sleeping saloon No. 111 as turned out in March 1883 with oil lighting and chain brake, although the photograph seems to have been taken after some months in service. Strangely, the only indication of the running number seems to be on the small white plates on the solebar over each axlebox. These plates were by no means generally fitted, but can be discerned on a number of photographs of other vehicles, particularly Post Offices.
   Like so many other carriages saloon 111 had a chequered career. In 1892 it was reconstructed on a bogie underframe and changes were made to the interior fittings. It was supplemented in 1902 and in the following year was rebuilt as a third-class dining saloon (without kitchen), incorporating a clerestory roof and electric lighting, with seats for 26 passengers. Late in 1914 it was again rebuilt to include a kitchen and pantry and in this form was included in Home Ambulance Train No. 9. It appears as No. 2111A on Page 44 of the 1915 *Diagram Book*. The vehicle was repainted in March 1919, but seems to have done little work thereafter; it had been broken up by the grouping.

There is also some doubt about the colour of the bolection mouldings around the fixed windows; some authorities specify that they were painted venetian red, to match the teak or mahogany droplight frames, and from the evidence of contemporary models and colour paintings it seems certain that this was so until about 1912. On LNWR carriages built from 1911 onwards with the 'toplight' style of panelling, the bolection mouldings were lake. The position regarding carriages with the 'Wolverton traditional' style of panelling repainted after 1911 is less clear. One observer about 1920 is certain that the bolection mouldings were lake on all carriages, while another is equally certain that on at least some vehicles they were venetian red; the contemporary paint-shop employees are unanimous

91

in specifying lake for the LNWR, but in addition one claims that venetian red was retained for the WCJS. The most consistent explanation is that a change of practice took place when the 'toplight' stock was introduced in 1911, but the time required for the whole fleet to be completely repainted, coupled with arrears brought about by the war, meant that the bolection mouldings on a proportion of the stock were still venetian red into the 1920s. This would apply particularly to the supplementary stock (which was normally touched up rather than given a full repaint), and also to vehicles which were new or repainted just before the change of practice occurred. On the 12-wheeled carriages, the dining and sleeping saloons and the WCJS 1909 stock, the fixed lights were held in flat frames of varnished teak, in the same manner as the door droplights of ordinary stock. This teak, incidentally, was Burma teak, of a medium to dark brown colour similar to mahogany, and not the West African timber commonly used nowadays for furniture. With the cove-roofed carriages of 1903, the door droplights on ordinary stock were of varnished bay-wood, and consequently exhibited a reddish tone.

The end steps of the carriage were picked out in black, but the metal part of corridor gangways was lake. The handrails mounted on the carriage ends and the short handrails on the roof over the end steps were painted terracotta, a colour with more orange in it than venetian red; the same colour was applied to the horizontal handrails which were

Plate 91   *National Railway Museum (Crown Copyright)*

Lavatory tri-composite No. 469 was the pioneer carriage of a batch of 65 built between 1886 and 1889 at the start of the Park regime. It has the later pattern 42' radial underframe with modified suspension to the centre wheelsets. The photograph was taken when the carriage was new with grease axleboxes, long lower stepboard, early gas lamp tops, no roof ventilators and rings along the edge of the roof for the Harrison train alarm system. Early vehicles to this design had 2'2" wide doors to the first-class compartments, but in 1887 the standard door width became 2' as on the inferior classes.

The carriage is in standard livery for the period; until the revised design of cornice made its appearance in 1887 the edge of the roof (and the arc of the roof as viewed from the end) were painted white — thereafter these surfaces were lake. The underframe, including the hornplates and the ends of the headstocks, is fully lined out, and the design of the etched glass lavatory window is clearly brought out.

In 1892-3 forty of these carriages were altered to provide lavatory facilities for the inferior classes (D161) and around 1906 nine of the remainder had the luggage box converted into a guard's brake compartment (D229). No. 463 remained on D165 as originally built and became 2865 in 1910. It had been supplemented by 1915 and survived long enough to receive LMS livery and its new duplicate series number 08080 in September 1923 — one of the first ex-LNWR vehicles to do so. Its withdrawal date is not known but it had gone by 1933.

fitted along the waist mouldings of all brake vans. The locking handles on the corridor gangways were also painted terracotta. Door and commode handles were polished brass.

The standard style of lettering on the door waist panel which specified the compartment class was originally introduced in 1874, and was gold outlined with a $\frac{1}{8}$" black line; at some stage after 1906, almost certainly at the time of the general renumbering of 1910-12,

92

a change was made to yellow letters. The initial letters 'F', 'S', 'T', and 'G' were $2\frac{5}{16}''$ high and the other letters $1\frac{13}{16}''$ high. The vertical strokes of the gold or yellow colour were $\frac{1}{2}''$ thick, and the horizontals $\frac{3}{8}''$. Numerals were $2\frac{7}{8}''$ in height and were also originally rendered in gold. Carriage running numbers were invariably displayed on the quarterlight panels twice on each side of the carriage. WCJS numerals were shaded in different colours of green, brown and white to simulate a blocking effect. On most LNWR carriages the numerals were simply outlined in black, but on royal and other special saloons more elaborate transfers were used, similar in style to the WCJS numerals but with red rather than green as the predominant shading colour. The numerals on these vehicles remained gold up to the grouping, although for ordinary LNWR numerals yellow replaced gold at the time of the 1910 renumbering. Third-class carriages were not affected by the renumbering, and consequently gold numerals were doubtless found in service somewhat later than the end of 1913, by which time the other classes of vehicle had been almost completely dealt with. The WCJS also is believed to have had gold numerals until the grouping. Certainly, gold powder, a finely powdered alloy of copper, aluminium and zinc, was still being purchased as late as November 1922.

On the London suburban electric stock the class designation was indicated by a white roundel placed on the centre of the longlight windows; the roundel was 6″ in diameter with the numeral '1' or '3' in white on a transparent ground. The word 'SMOKING' was superimposed in red over the numeral where appropriate; in those days smoking was permitted only in compartments specially designated.

In addition to the capital stock fleet of carriages, the LNWR (but not the WCJS) maintained a considerable number of 'supplementary' or duplicate stock vehicles. These had been replaced in the capital stock by newer vehicles but, except in the accountancy sense, were by no means 'life-expired' and were often to be found in regular service, albeit on secondary duties. Before 1910, transfer to the supplementary list was normally indicated by adding 2000 to the vehicle's existing number, but about 1890 the capital stock of third-class carriages reached 2000 and thereafter supplementary thirds were renumbered by adding 3000 (in a few cases, 4000 or 5000) to their existing numbers. Vehicles which were supplemented after the 1910 renumbering scheme were given an 0 prefix to their 1910 series numbers, while those which were already in the supplementary list had an A suffix

Plate 92 *(G.H.Platt collection)*
50′ corridor brake composite No. 254 at Euston in 1899 when it was about two years old. Originally brake third No. 2293 the two compartments at the far end were soon re-designated second class, and the carriage was duly renumbered as 254 in the composite series. However, within a year it reverted to a brake third and was again renumbered 709. It became 7119 in the 1910 renumbering scheme, and around 1920 was converted into a three-compartment end-brake vehicle to D317, electric light being installed at the same time. Its LMS numbers were 6839 and later 6007, and it was withdrawn in January 1936. As seen here, the coats of arms are displayed on the outer compartment doors, a practice which seems to have been usual before the turn of the century.

added to their existing 2xxx series numbers. The livery carried by the supplementary stock was in all respects the same as that of the capital stock, but as supplementary carriages had only a limited life expectancy, they rarely received full repaints.

Normally, all carriages displayed the coat of arms twice on each side, on the lower panels (they were not true arms as they had not been granted by the heraldic authorities). Like all LNWR armorial transfers, they featured Britannia with a lion; the carriage version was 9½″ wide and 9½″ deep. Until the start of the Park regime in 1886, and also for a short period around the turn of the century in the case of corridor stock, they were frequently placed on the compartment doors, but otherwise it was normal to mount the transfers on the body between the doors. These transfers were made with real gold leaf, and when a vehicle was completely repainted the old transfers were scraped off, and the gold content recovered for resale. Until 1910 passenger-carrying vehicles also carried the elaborately intertwined gold-leaf letters 'LNWR' or 'WCJS' in the form of a monogram, 9″ long and 3¼″ high. Until about 1899 it usually appeared twice on each side of the carriage, but only once thereafter. In November 1874 the locomotive committee had ordered 'the West Coast arms and monogram to be painted on all WCJS passenger stock including the third class carriages', which implies that these adornments were not generally used even on composite coaches until this time. Gold or yellow block letters 'WCJS' or 'L&NWR' were also positioned in the waist panel of the ogees on those brake vans with a central guard's compartment, but never on passenger-carrying stock or on brake vans with an end-guard arrangement. These block letters were used instead of the monograms which consequently did not appear on centre-guard brake vans. The side lamps mounted on the ogees were painted red.

Until about 1890 carriage underframes were painted the same lake as the bodies and lined out; this applied to solebars, hornplates, headstocks and buffer guides, other parts

Plate 93   *National Railway Museum (Crown Copyright)*
One of the earliest carriages to be built on the radial underframe was this 5 1/2 compartment first No. 165 which was turned out from Wolverton works in 1884, although the frames were made at Crewe. Only four were built, and they were originally included in set trains for working between London and Liverpool/Manchester; the absence of lavatory accommodation led to their rapid displacement from the main line, however, and they ended up in suburban sets in the Liverpool District. No. 165 became 4618 in the 1910 renumbering and was supplemented (0 prefix) in the following year; the date of withdrawal is not known but was probably a year or two before the grouping.
The photograph was taken in 1901 (note the modern type of train alarm apparatus introduced in 1899) and shows the early pattern of radial underframe. Oil axleboxes have replaced the original grease pattern and the long lower step-board has been removed except for a short section at the right-hand end of each side.
The body of the carriage is 8′6″ wide and thus comparatively rare. Note the seven rubber support pads spaced along the solebar. Other details worth examining include the blue 'Smoking' labels, the ring-pattern door handles, the couplings, and the dimension plate at the right-hand end of the solebar. These plates were moved to the body end from 1914. The carriage was originally oil lit but converted to gas a year or so after construction. The torpedo ventilators were added around 1895.

such as gas cylinders being black. Thereafter the whole of the underframe was painted unlined black and varnished; it is thought that this change coincided with the decision to discontinue radial underframes in favour of bogie construction. The wooden centres of Mansell wheels were painted brown and varnished, but the steel wheels introduced in 1913 were black.

Clerestory sides and carriage roofs were officially white at all times, but several photographs show brand-new vehicles with light or dark grey roofs. In any case, the effects of smoke and dirt rapidly changed the colour to dark grey or black. Even when the body of a coach was completely stripped down and repainted, which occurred about every five or six years, it was not usual to repaint the roof unless it required special attention. Roof fittings were normally the same colour as the roof, but in the 1890 – 1900 period it was not unusual to paint the gas lamp tops and torpedo ventilators black, which consequently stood out prominently on the white roof. Until 1887 the guttering along the edge of the cantrail, and the arc of the roof as viewed from the end of the carriage, were painted the roof colour, but in that year a redesigned cornice made its appearance and thereafter these surfaces were lake.

From 1886 the waist panel in the double luggage doors of all cupboards and brake compartments was made of slate for chalking the destinations of the contents. Before that time, the word 'LUGGAGE' appeared on one of the doors. Where the double doors served as the guard's door as well, that is, were the only entrance to the guard's compartment, the waist panel in the right-hand door was slated, and the other was painted white with the legend 'GUARD' in the usual way, but after 1900 the waist panel on this door too was often changed to slate. The waist panels on the sliding doors of parcels, milk and most fish vans were also of slate, but four-wheeled covered carriage trucks had a slate panel fitted centrally in the upper section of the door.

Until about 1903, smoking compartments had the word 'SMOKING' under their class designation, making two lines of lettering in the waist panel, thus: 'FIRST/SMOKING'. Naturally, these were rendered in characters smaller than standard. A minute of August 1888 had previously called for the removal of the words 'SMOKING COMPARTMENT' from the doors of composite carriages for main-line traffic, but how these words were rendered is uncertain. Coaching stock painted in the full passenger livery, such as parcels vans, usually had the letters 'L&NWR', the vehicle's number and often the purpose of the vehicle in gold or gold-coloured characters, outlined in black when on a white ground. Position and wording varied widely.

Second-class accommodation ceased to be provided on WCJS services from 1st May 1893, and was finally abandoned on the LNWR from 1st January 1912. In most cases the former second-class compartments were downgraded to third, and LNWR seconds, and second- and third-class composites, were renumbered into the third-class or brake-third series. The alteration of the compartment designation was achieved by fixing a white

95

Plate 95 *(G.H.Platt collection)*

An excellent close-up taken at about the turn of the century of 30′1″ third No. 2004, complete with vintage guard. It has lettering in gold rather than gold colour, and ring-pattern door handles. In all, 827 vehicles were built of this type, the largest number ever built by a British railway to the same design, though many underwent various conversions later. No. 2004 was built in 1892 and withdrawn in 1935 as LMS No. 26385.

Plate 96 *(G.H.Platt collection)*

The same guard poses in front of an unidentified vehicle dating from the 1870s — note the sunken quarterlight frames with rounded corners and the polished wood droplight frame. The two visible compartments have been downgraded from first to second class; at various times, particularly in the last century, strenuous attempts were made to adjust the accommodation offered to the somewhat variable pattern of demand, and carriages changed from firsts to composites to thirds and back again (with consequential renumbering in the appropriate series) with bewildering frequency. This vehicle is still oil-lit and the Harrison cord is in use.

Plate 97 *(G.H.Platt collection)*

Although most carriages were repainted in LMS colours by 1927, a few survivors retained the old livery for many years longer. This photograph was taken in October 1937, about six months after official withdrawal. The carriage is No. 03436, a 42′ luggage composite to D161 which was built in 1889 as No. 1200. It had been supplemented by 1923 — the 0 prefix is simply applied in front of the existing number. The vehicle was allotted LMS numbers 08002 and later 19388 but obviously never carried them.

plate with the word 'THIRD' thereon in the usual style over the existing word 'SECOND', and was thus accomplished more or less overnight. By contrast, vehicles involved in renumbering schemes acquired their new numbers only at the next repaint, except in the case of vehicles transferred to the supplementary stock where the A suffix or 0 prefix was transferred on locally. The first carriage to receive its new number under the 1910 renumbering scheme (5718 of D215) did so on 9th April, and by the end of the year 1336 of the 6643 vehicles involved in the renumbering had been dealt with. By the end of 1911 3193 had been renumbered, and by 12th May 1912 3906, the last total available. Only a handful remained with their old numbers by the end of 1913, and the renumbering appears to have been completed on 20th May 1914.

The newly formed LMS decided on 31st May 1923 to adopt the crimson lake colour scheme of the Midland Railway, a photograph of 'the first train in the new colours' being taken at Wolverton early in September. The last new vehicle to carry LNWR livery was turned out on 18th October 1923. With a normal painting cycle of five to six years, the old liveries remained in diminishing use until about 1930, but a few vehicles with a limited life expectancy were still in the old colours until their final withdrawal in the mid-1930s.

Plate 98 *(G.H.Platt collection)*
Traditionally styled 57′×9′ double-ended tri-composite slip carriage No. 1286 of D205 was built in 1908, but it is not clear whether the photograph (at Euston) was taken when it was new or not. The white tyres would suggest so, but in this case the roof must have been grey from the start. Two compartments were provided for each of the three classes. The roof board is permanently mounted. The carriage later became LNWR 6106 and LMS 9551; it was withdrawn in 1951 as LMS 7125.

Plates 99/100/101 *(G.H.Platt collection)*
These three photographs show the side and both ends of steam railmotor car No. 1, apparently as turned out new in 1905. The roof is clearly grey rather than white, and the painting of the cornice and roof arc stands out clearly. Contrary to normal practice the waist panels in the luggage doors are not slated, but have the word 'LUGGAGE' applied to the left-hand door. There was, of course, no need to make provision for chalking the destination on these doors.

97

Plate 102 *(G.H.Platt collection)*
This view of Home Ambulance Train No. 19 was presumably taken when it was completed in December 1915. The first vehicle is guard, medical and nurses car No. 5320 which was built new for this purpose, and after the war was converted into an invalid saloon on D55. The second vehicle is dining saloon No. 2100A which had started life in March 1882 as the pioneer radial carriage, sleeping saloon No 100. It had been altered to a third-class dining saloon in 1903 (which included fitting a clerestory to the roof) and was further altered for ambulance train use by converting part of the seating area into a kitchen and pantry, and fitting electric lighting. This vehicle was not reinstated after the war, and its body was sold in April 1921. The third vehicle is ward car No. 8871 which was also newly built for this train, and ultimately became a brake van on D378C. *continued over page*

continued from previous page

The next six vehicles are all ward cars which have been heavily reconstructed from brake vans of D376 — in order they are 8016, 8087, 8089, 8012, 8146 and 8177. D376 consisted of ten brake vans which apart from the cove-roof profile were identical to the earlier examples of the corresponding (and much more numerous) high-roof design D375. This combination of 8′6″ width and 7′10″ body height made them particularly suitable for ambulance use as they cleared more restricted loading gauges than that of the LNWR. All of these ward cars were reinstated as brake vans after the war, still nominally on D376 although no reversal of the structural alterations (provision of side windows and removal of guards' ogees) was carried out. Far in the distance, the last vehicle is brake and stores car 07158, originally one of the 8′6″ wide brake thirds built in 1884 for the London-Liverpool services. It had been converted to a corridor vehicle in 1897 and a small kitchen was included in the guard's compartment. The train retains its normal LNWR livery as it was used exclusively within Britain — ambulance trains destined for the Continent were repainted in khaki. The Geneva crosses on the sides were of course red. The white roofs seem to disregard the possibility of aerial bombardment by Zeppelins!

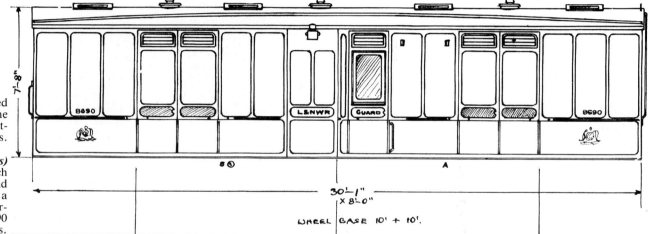

These drawings were prepared by J.P.Richards and show the general style and position of lettering on a variety of vehicles.

Figure 25 *(J.P.Richards)* 30′1″ brake van D385, of which 354 were built between 1889 and 1898, later versions having a number of differences, particularly the underframes. 8690 is from one of the final batches.

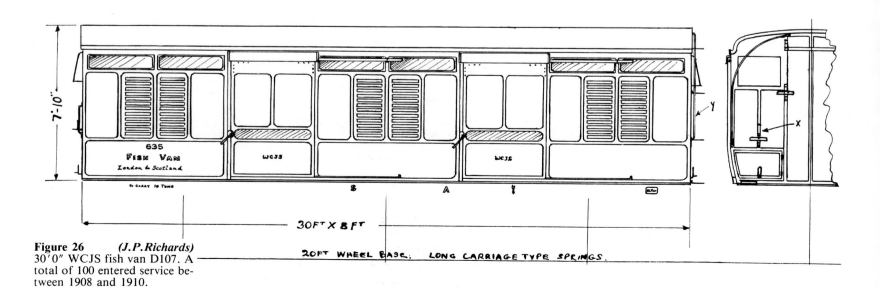

Figure 26 *(J.P.Richards)* 30′0″ WCJS fish van D107. A total of 100 entered service between 1908 and 1910.

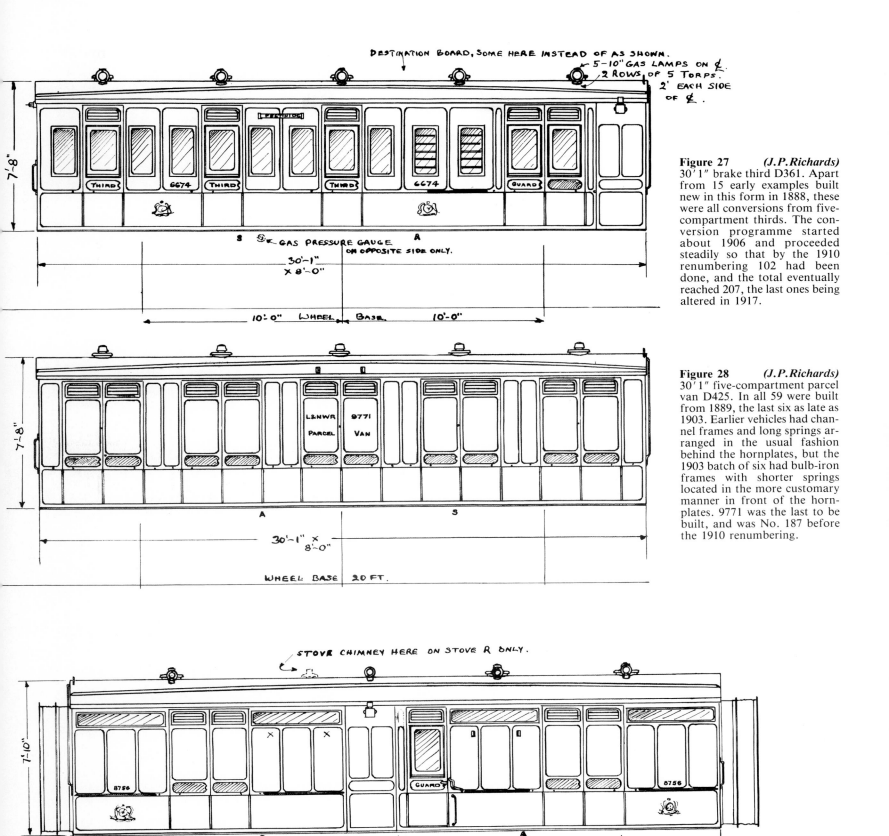

DESTINATION BOARD, SOME HERE INSTEAD OF AS SHOWN.
5-10" GAS LAMPS ON ₵
2 ROWS OF 5 TORPS.
2' EACH SIDE OF ₵.

7'-8"

THIRD   6674   THIRD   THIRD   6674   GUARD

GAS PRESSURE GAUGE ON OPPOSITE SIDE ONLY.

30'-1" X 8'-0"

10'-0"   WHEEL   BASE.   10'-0"

Figure 27 *(J.P.Richards)*
30'1" brake third D361. Apart from 15 early examples built new in this form in 1888, these were all conversions from five-compartment thirds. The conversion programme started about 1906 and proceeded steadily so that by the 1910 renumbering 102 had been done, and the total eventually reached 207, the last ones being altered in 1917.

7'-8"

L&NWR 9771
Parcel Van

A   S

30'-1" X 8'-0"

WHEEL BASE   20 FT.

Figure 28 *(J.P.Richards)*
30'1" five-compartment parcel van D425. In all 59 were built from 1889, the last six as late as 1903. Earlier vehicles had channel frames and long springs arranged in the usual fashion behind the hornplates, but the 1903 batch of six had bulb-iron frames with shorter springs located in the more customary manner in front of the hornplates. 9771 was the last to be built, and was No. 187 before the 1910 renumbering.

STOVE CHIMNEY HERE ON STOVE R ONLY.

7'-10"

8756   GUARD   8756

S   A

32 FT X 8 FT 6"

DYNAMO DRIVEN OFF THIS AXLE.   GUARDS DOOR OPENS INWARDS, HENCE NO RUBBER STOPS.

22 FT WHEEL BASE.   LONG CARRIAGE SPRINGS

Figure 29 *(J.P.Richards)*
32' milk traffic brake van D384. 40 of these rather handsome cove-roofed vehicles were constructed in 1907, Nos. 752 to 791, increased by 8000 at the renumbering. 8755 was destroyed in the Abermule accident of 1915 but the remainder reached the grouping as LMS 2791-2829.

Figure 30 *(J.P.Richards)*
42' brake van D382. A total of 164 were built between 1911 and 1921, all with 8xxx series numbers from new. The first 24, including 8210, were gas lit while the remainder had electric lighting. The design marked the change away from the centre-guard arrangement, which with few exceptions had been standard LNWR practice from the early 1870s, to the end-guard layout.

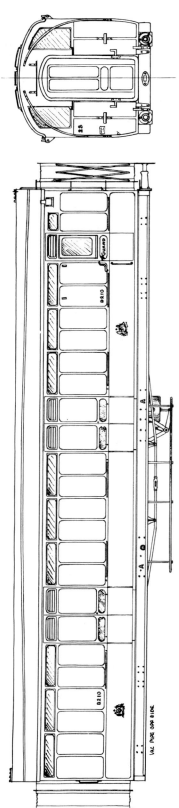

Figure 31 *(J.P.Richards)*
42' brake van D383. These vans were a shorter version of the very common 50' vans of D375, which in turn derived from previous cove and arc roof designs. 40 vehicles, all gas lit, were built in 1910-11, and all had 8xxx series numbers from new. The LMS converted much gas-lit stock to electric lighting in the late 1920s and early 1930s.

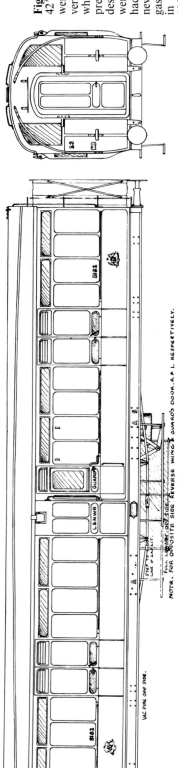

VAC. PIPE O/H/P SIDE.

Figure 32 *(J.P.Richards)*
50' brake van D375. In all 177 of these were built between 1907 and 1910; later batches had three toplights over each section of six panels as illustrated, but the first 40 vans (which included 367, later 8367) built in 1907 had only two — the van in the drawing thus bears an incorrect number. The design was a simple development of D376 which had a cove roof but was otherwise identical to the earlier batches of D375 vehicles. Originally gas lit, many were altered to electric lighting by the grouping, and further conversions were carried out by the LMS.

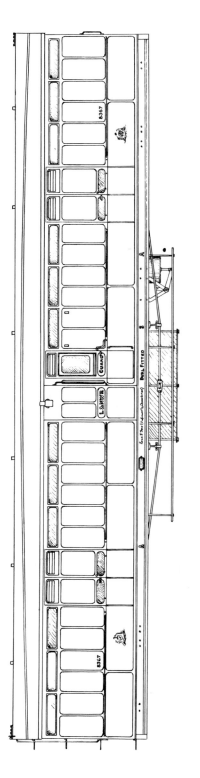

101

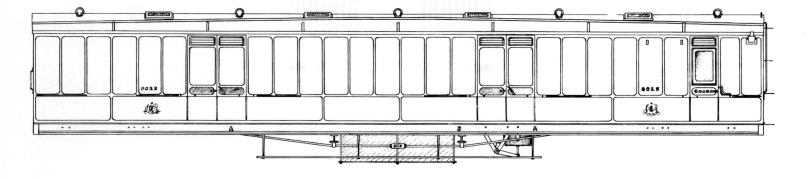

Figure 33 *(J.P.Richards)*
50' brake van D373. Seven of
these handsome cove-roof
vehicles were specially constructed in 1907 to run with the
contemporary 9' wide Euston-
Holyhead corridor sets on the
'Irish Mail' services. No. 25
(8025 after the renumbering)
was the pioneer vehicle. Two
more with high-roof profile and
toplights to D372 were built in
1908, to go with additional
Holyhead sets. Originally gas
lit, all but one had been altered
to electricity by the grouping,
and the vans remained in the
Holyhead sets for many years.

Saloons and Special Stock

Carriages built in the 'twelve-wheel' style of panelling exhibited a number of variations
from the ordinary livery style. On these vehicles the moulding along the bottom edge of
the carriage was rounded on both edges, and was fully lined out at each side. The recessed entrance doors on these vehicles were normally of unpainted varnished Burma teak
or mahogany, but this did not apply to the doors of brake vans or van ends in the 'American
Special' and 2pm 'Corridor' twelve-wheeled stock of 1907-9, which were painted in the
usual way. The doors of the later twelve-wheeled stock which were only slightly inset from
the body side were also painted normally.

The lettering and numbering on saloons and special vehicles also differed from that
on ordinary stock. The 34' dining saloons of 1889 had 'DINING SALOON' and the
number at waist level in rather large and ornate gilt serif letters, which were blocked in
white, shading to red below and to the left, and countershaded in black to the right, and
were about $4\frac{1}{2}''$ high as near as can be estimated. The succeeding 42' diners for the Manchester service had the words in larger letters in the form of an arc on the lower part of
the body sides. The 1892 WCJS dining saloon sets had the designation displayed above
the windows in ornamental gilt lettering, shaded in green rather than red as above, and
also $4\frac{1}{2}''$ high, while the number, originally once only, was located in the centre of one
of the panels between the windows in approximately 3'' figures. The earliest 65'6'' saloons
had the same lettering at first, but the number now also appeared on the cantrail at each
end of the vehicle in the same size of characters. From 1898, however, with detail changes
in design, all lettering was placed on the waist panel in shaded block letters about $2\frac{5}{8}''$
high with initial letters a little larger, nearer 3''.

The body of LNWR sleeping saloon No. 2112A was sold in 1921 for use as a holiday
bungalow and in 1980 was repurchased for eventual restoration. At that time the numerals
were still clearly visible. Remarkably, the carriage retained the ornate serif characters,

Plate 103 *(G.H.Platt collection)*

Dining saloon No. 5026 was one of three built to D37 in 1914 and although described as 'third class' both in the building register and the diagram book appear to have been effectively 'unclassed' and used mainly as composites.

painted in yellow (not gold) with shading in black and red, the latter fading through pink into white. The numerals were $4\frac{5}{8}''$ high, inclusive of $\frac{3}{4}''$ shading, while the 'A' was $2\frac{3}{8}''$ high inclusive of $\frac{1}{2}''$ shading. It is thus probable that this style of numeral was retained for the early sleeping and dining saloons until their final withdrawal.

Post offices carried their insignia high up on one of the white panels above the waist, in the form of the block letters 'L&NWR' or 'WCJS' with the vehicle's number prefixed by 'No.' immediately below. Transfers were always gilt. They also carried the royal coat of arms in place of the railway company's and usually displayed the legend 'V (Crown) R POST OFFICE' immediately to the left of the entrance doors. After 1901 this was naturally replaced by 'E (Crown) R' and after 1910 by the insignia of King George V. Where a late-fee letter-box was provided, the box itself or the panel with the letter-box slot was painted GPO red. Gilt lettering shaded black 1″ high proclaimed the need for an additional $\frac{1}{2}$d stamp on letters posted in the box.

There were two variations from the ordinary passenger carriage livery. Four-wheeled carriages used on the Broad Street – Mansion House 'Outer Circle' service built from 1890 were finished in varnished dark Burma teak as this was found to withstand the sulphurous atmospheric conditions on the sub-surface lines better than paint. The stock was unlined and class designations were in the form of a large '1', '2' or '3' on the lower panel of the doors in place of the usual wording. On the previous generation of carriages the white upper panels had been abandoned in 1884 in favour of all-lake, apart from a trial with a special white paint in 1886 which was not successful. After service in France during the war, these vehicles returned to the UK and were rebuilt as 56′ bogie carriages by joining two of the four-wheelers together on a new underframe. In this form they carried the ordinary passenger two-colour livery.

Carriages demoted to the supplementary stock normally retained their two-colour livery, but very elderly carriages used for workmen's trains, for example in South Wales, were painted purple-brown all over in the same way as horseboxes and trucks, unlined and with plain yellow letters; this also applied to old stock which had been appropriated for permanent way personnel and breakdown-train tool or riding vans.

The LNWR royal saloons of 1903 were described in the *Railway Engineer* as follows:- 'The exterior of the saloons are painted the standard L&NW colours, but particular care has been given to the painting and varnishing, with the result that it would be impossible to find a finer piece of work anywhere in the country. The waist panels are ornamented with the Royal Arms and the collars of some of the Royal Orders. The entire length of the cornice is carved with an oak leaf design and gilded. The entrance door frames are lined with polished brass, which sets off the polished mahogany doors. The door and commode handles are handsomely carved and gold plated. The commode handles are massive and terminate with lion's heads. The ends of the head-stocks are covered with gilded lion's heads. The bogie springs and axle-boxes are painted chocolate colour picked out with yellow, and the edge of the tyres are painted white, the retaining rings black, and the teak centres of the wheels are polished.'

103

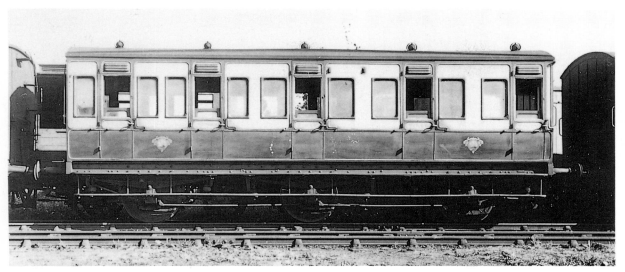

Plate 104 *(G.H.Platt collection)*
The Dundalk, Newry & Greenore Railway retained the LNWR livery until the GNR(I) took over in 1953. Composite No. 2 seen at Dundalk in 1950 was one of two built in 1909 — the other (No.1) is now preserved in the Belfast Transport Museum. The two-and-a-half compartments on the right are first class and the remaining two compartments are second class.

Plate 105 *(G.H.Platt collection)*
Corridor brake third No. 6725, built in 1913 to D307 and photographed about 1921 when it was running as part of Inter-Corridor Set No. 13. Inter-Corridor sets were assembled from mid-1919 and were almost invariably of four carriages formed from 57′0″ BTK, 57′0″ CK, 52′6″ CK and 57′0″ BTK of various diagrams. The actual composition of the sets changed very frequently, however.

Plate 106 *(G.H.Platt collection*
The elaborate LNWR monogram which was displayed on all passenger vehicles until 1910.

Plate 107 *(G.H.Platt collection)*

Saloon No. 5179 started life in 1892 as one of four corridor sleeping saloons which were operated as pairs on the 'Irish Mail' service. Nos. 178 and 179 ran as a pair and were badly damaged in the Norton Bridge accident on 8th December 1899 but were subsequently reconstructed. All four were converted into inspection saloons in 1913 and 5179 (which was the Chief Civil Engineer, Mr. Ford's saloon) appears on D6 in the diagram book. It became LMS No. 10683 at the grouping and lasted well into BR days as 45013. The number is displayed only on the two oval white plates on the solebar, a practice which seems to have been invariable for inspection saloons and not uncommon with other saloons, at any rate in the last century. Also, the roof is quite plainly grey.

Plate 108 *(G.H.Platt collection)*

Parcel van No. 09667 of D417 was photographed about 1920 and shows the normal lettering arrangement for parcels and similar vans. The vehicle is unusual in that the sides are quite flat without any 'tumblehome' below the waist. A total of 12 of this type were built in 1884/5, dimensions being 32' × 8' × 7'4" and the low roof is apparent in comparison with the adjacent vehicles. They were originally fitted with side (Lansdowne) gangways but about 1901 were altered to centre gangways. Four were appropriated for use in the St Helens stores train in 1904, and a few years later most if not all the remainder were fitted for use as pigeon vans. Supplemented around 1916 No. 09667 became LMS 02143 but the whole class was extinct by 1933.

Horseboxes, Fish Vans, Carriage Trucks and Similar Vehicles

In the last century it is believed that carriage trucks (whether open or covered) and horseboxes were painted in carriage lake, but after about 1900 they were painted in a colour known as 'quick brown'. This colour was made from a mixture of indian red and black (possibly with the addition of a quantity of burnt turkey umber) and was probably the same as was used for undercoating on the passenger vehicles. At a distance, this dark chocolate colour was barely distinguishable from the lake of the carriages, but at a closer range it was less lustrous and transparent. The colour was in fact a dark purple brown which was intended as a close approximation of the expensive lake.

Until about 1916, when economies brought about by the First World War forced it to be discontinued, lining was applied to horseboxes, trucks and similar vehicles in the form of a single ⅜" yellow line to the edges of all mouldings. The louvred door ventilators were also lined on their lower edge, while yellow lining was also applied to the edges of the ironwork which formed the hinges of the doors to the horse compartment. An official photograph (Plate 110) of one horsebox shows a white line similar to that used on passenger stock around the ends and bottom of the body, but others do not. The vehicles carried their running numbers once only, placed centrally on the doors to the horse compartment. Plain block letters were used, yellow before about 1916, white after, but some vehicles such as the 27' motor car vans carried large 'gold-coloured' serif letters. Car-

Plate 109 *(G.H.Platt collection)*
Evidence of lettering styles in the Victorian era is inevitably scanty, and this photograph is correspondingly valuable. It shows the lettering carried by horsebox No. 200, a 14'3" long vehicle built in 1870. It was replaced in the capital stock by a new 21' horsebox in 1890, and was accordingly transferred to the supplementary stock by the addition of 2000 to its number. The date of withdrawal is not known, but was 1897 at the latest. Its body was sold and survived until about 1960 when this photograph was taken by G.N.Ibbott. The characters are in serif rather than the later block style, and the 2 prefix has been added in front of the existing number. The lettering is recorded as being in gold as opposed to yellow. It is more than likely that this represents the style used when Richard Bore was at Wolverton, and that the change to block letters took place under Park, but unhappily no further details are known.

riage and fish trucks were also lined and usually displayed their capacity, for example, *'To carry 5 Tons'*, in small italic script, which style was also used for such information as *'To be returned to Euston'*, but in later years block letters were used. The company's initials were always rendered as 'L&NWR', with an ampersand.

Before about 1900, fruit, milk and fish vans (but not covered trucks) which were constructed similarly to passenger vehicles, were painted in the passenger style, but thereafter they were all-brown, with yellow lining.

By about 1905 milk vans which had been converted from old brake vans in the supplementary stock were also brown. The WCJS fish vans of 1908 carried their running numbers once only, centrally on the lower panel at the left-hand end of the van; below the number appeared the words 'FISH VAN' in block letters and *'London & Scotland'* in either italic or block script. As built, a WCJS monogram appeared on each of the two

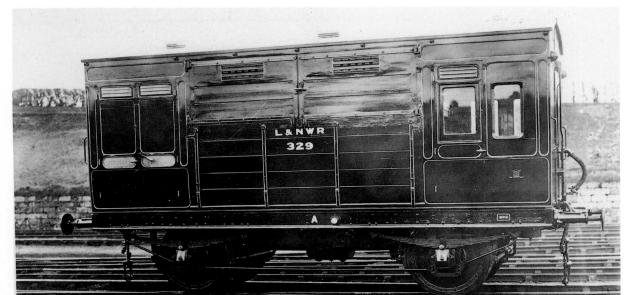

Plate 110 *(G.H.Platt collection)*
Horsebox No. 329 was one of the exceedingly numerous examples of D436, of which no less than 681 were built in the period 1890 to 1906, with a further 11 in 1913, after which construction of horseboxes ceased entirely. No. 329 itself was built in 1901 after the change from channel-section to bulb-iron frames had taken place. No handbrake is fitted and it would seem that the photograph was taken when the vehicle was new (white roof). The white line along the bottom moulding, and at the extreme ends, seems to have been discontinued later, perhaps as a wartime economy. No. 329 became 10329 at the 1910 renumbering, and later LMS 3485.

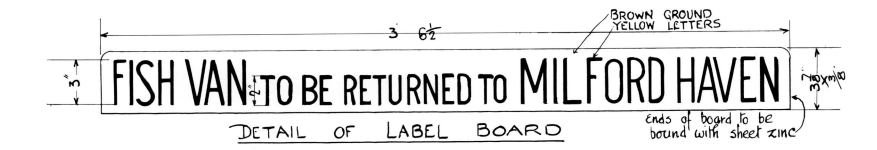

BROWN GROUND
YELLOW LETTERS

3' 6½"

3"

2"

30 × m⊗

FISH VAN TO BE RETURNED TO MILFORD HAVEN

Ends of board to be
bound with sheet zinc

DETAIL OF LABEL BOARD

Figure 34
This Wolverton drawing of October 1921 shows the new label boards for fruit and milk vans and combination trucks which had been re-allocated to fish traffic, as well as the previous writing which was to be painted out.

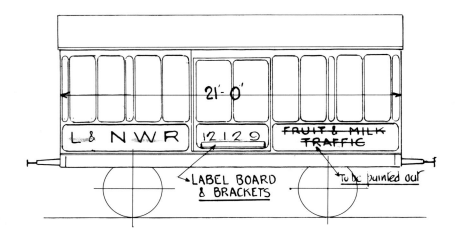

21' 0"

L & N W R   12129   FRUIT & MILK TRAFFIC

LABEL BOARD
& BRACKETS

To be painted out

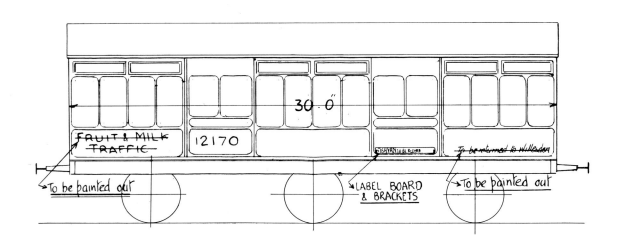

30' 0"

FRUIT & MILK TRAFFIC   12170   FISH VAN to be returned   To be returned to Willesden

To be painted out   LABEL BOARD & BRACKETS   To be painted out

sliding doors, but no coat of arms was applied. There were a number of exceptions to the general rules, in particular the royal double-horsebox No. 700 and the royal fourgon truck No. 100, both of which carried the full passenger livery.

About 1913 the LNWR began to paint 'FRUIT & MILK TRAFFIC' in large letters on the side of covered trucks allocated to that traffic; the vehicle's number was also displayed in 8″ figures and in the case of 21′ trucks the company's initials 'L&NWR' as well in 10″ figures. All this lettering was in white. In October 1921 all 25 of the fruit and milk vans to D454, and 24 combination trucks to D445A, were reassigned as fish vans for Milford Haven traffic, and were relettered as shown in Fig 43. Each vehicle was provided with two label boards as detailed in the drawing, and the words FRUIT & MILK TRAFFIC were painted out.

Gas reservoir wagons were black, with the number and 'L&NWR' in white.

Private Trucks

A number of covered carriage trucks were permanently allocated for the use of private traders, mainly manufacturers of road carriages and motor cars. They were painted in the normal LNWR livery but in addition were lettered with particulars of the firm. Although they were usually included in the same diagram as general-purpose carriage trucks of the same overall dimensions, these private trucks were often of special design and differed considerably in external appearance. Examples, taken from official Wolverton drawings, are included in Figs.33 to 40, although the precise layout of the lettering may have varied slightly in practice — in some cases two or more drawings were prepared, presumably so that the client could select the preferred version. It is a great pity that no photographs of these colourful and striking vehicles seem to have survived.

Six vehicles in the full passenger livery were also reserved for particular traffics, three 45′ newspaper vans for Messrs Wyman, two 30′1″ five-compartment parcels vans for Pryce Jones Ltd, and a similar van for Messrs Palethorpes sausages. They are illustrated by rather crude sketches which appear to have been drawn about 1906. The size and position of the lettering should not be interpreted too literally. According to an official drawing, the van allocated to Palethorpe's traffic carried permanently mounted roof boards, 25′ long, painted blue with white lettering, as follows:

MAKERS TO		OFFICES DUDLEY
H.M. THE QUEEN.	H. PALETHORPE'S ROYAL CAMBRIDGE SAUSAGE VAN	WORCESTERSHIRE.
2′6″	20′0″	2′6″

The lettering on the doors was arranged in one horizontal line, thus:-

SAUSAGES CREWE SAUSAGES MANCHESTER SAUSAGES NORMANTON

SAUSAGES HUDDERSFIELD SAUSAGES LEEDS.

Small letters 'To be returned to Euston' appeared at the bottom of the body at the left-hand side.

Figure 35
CCT No. 81 was 22′ by 7′10″ and was built in 1886 as a private truck for Messrs Lawtons of Liverpool. The drawing shows it as running in 1907 when perhaps the lettering was changed to reflect the changes in Lawton's business from horse to motor carriages. The truck was supplemented as 2081A in 1909 and did not survive the grouping. The livery was almost certainly LNWR brown with gold-coloured lettering.

Figure 36
Another drawing of 2081A was prepared in October 1914 showing the lettering to be applied. By now Lawtons have acquired over 200 first-class prize medals (presumably for vehicle bodies) and an evocative telegraphic address!

Figure 37
CTT No. 255 was also built to the unusual 22′ length in 1887 for the use of Morgan & Co Ltd. It was supplemented as 011255 in 1910-11 and was destroyed by fire at Long Buckby on 15th January 1918. A third 22′ CCT, No. 131, had been built in 1878 for Messrs Forder & Co Ltd — this one was supplemented as 2131 by 1906.

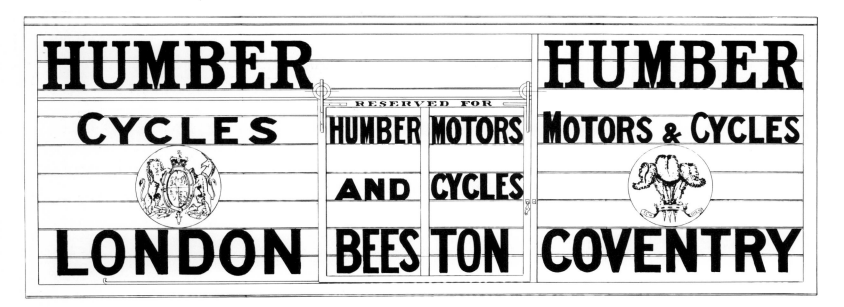

Figure 38
In 1904 a 21′ CCT was lettered for the use of Humber Cycles. The vehicle in question was apparently No. 181 which had been built to D448 in 1884. Of the 83 trucks constructed to this design at least 17 were allocated to private firms and many others were altered to milk trucks quite early on in their lives. No.181 duly became 11181 in the 1910 renumbering scheme and received its LMS number 4017 in November 1923; the final withdrawal date is unknown, but D448 was not extinct until 1937.

Figure 39
Another D448 example was No. 401 of 1891, and which seems to have been allocated to Anne Cowburn in June 1912, by which time it had been renumbered as 11401. It became LMS 4622 in March 1924, but it is not known how long its status as a private truck lasted — the practice may well have ceased by the grouping.

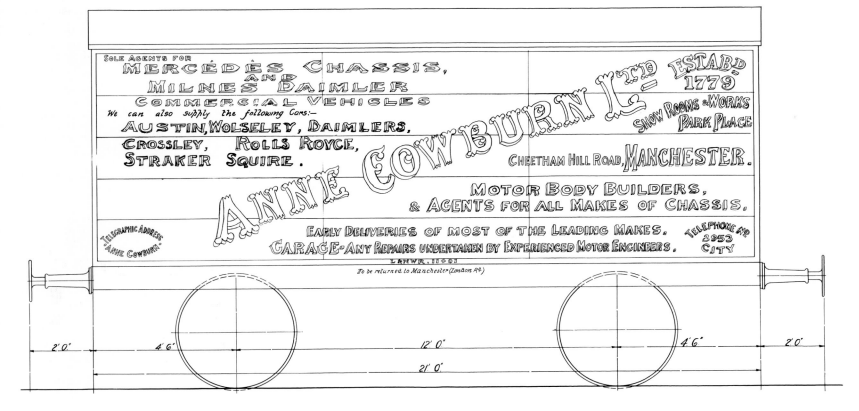

110

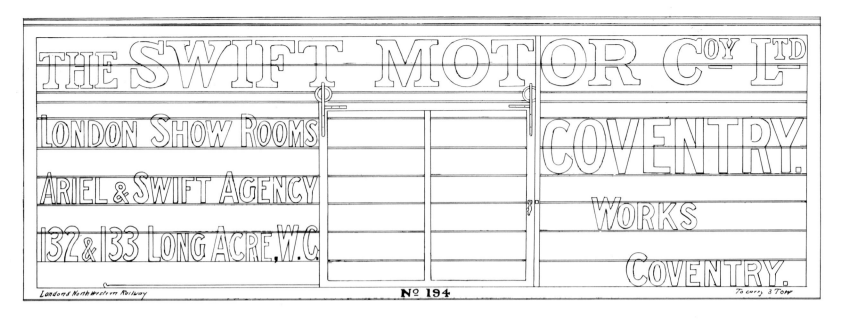

Figure 40
No.194 was also D448 of 1891 and built in the same batch as Cowburn's truck. In June 1904 it was allocated to the long-defunct Swift Motor Co Ltd. By the grouping it had been supplemented as 011194 but received its LMS duplicate series number 04042 in September 1923.

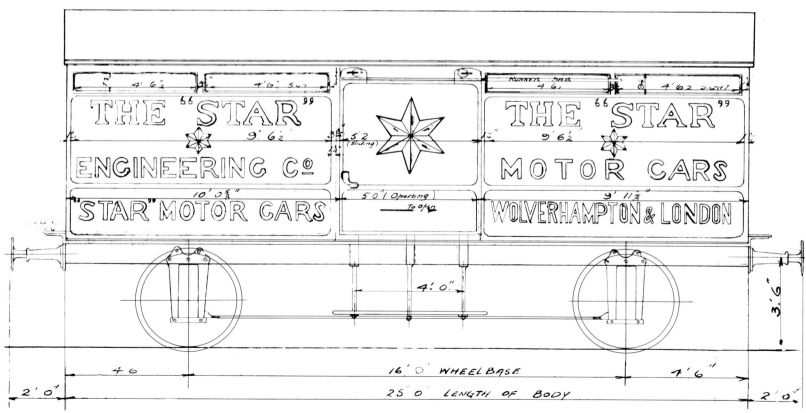

111

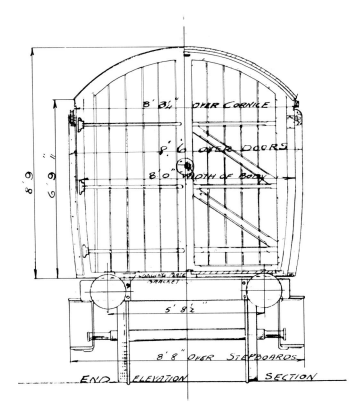

Figure 41
CCl No. 232 was to D447 and was specially built for the Star Engineering Co in 1906, 25′ long by 8′ wide and 8′10″ high to the top of the roof. In November 1923 it became LMS 4606, and in later years 37074 (subsequently 37660) — it was not withdrawn until December 1951, many years after its role as a private truck ceased. Another truck to this design, No. 600, was built in 1907 for the use of Forder & Co.

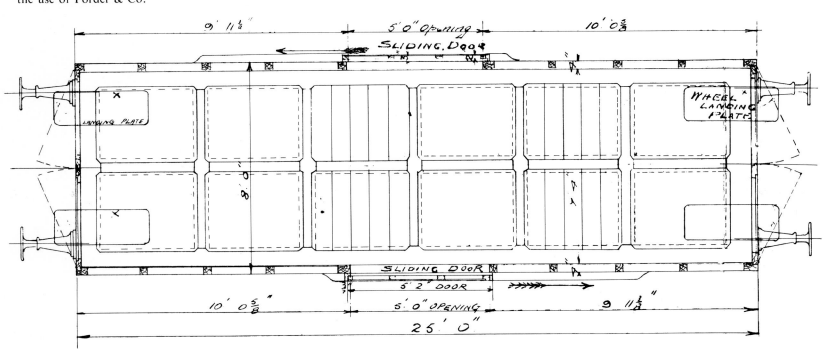

112

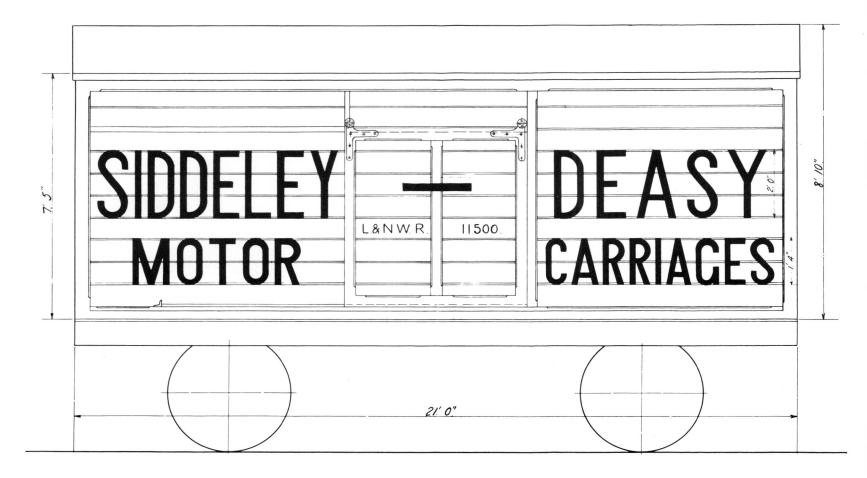

Figure 42
Yet another D448 example is No.11500 (originally No. 500), built in 1892 and repainted for use by Siddeley-Deasy in July 1914. It was allocated LMS 4631 at the grouping, but did not survive long enough to receive it. A modellers' drawing of this type of CCT may be found in *Model Railways* for November 1974.

Figure 43
These sketches are extremely crude, and are included only to give some idea of the liveries carried by private trucks — no other details survive. The sketches seem to have been drawn about 1906, perhaps as a first assignment for a junior draughtsman.

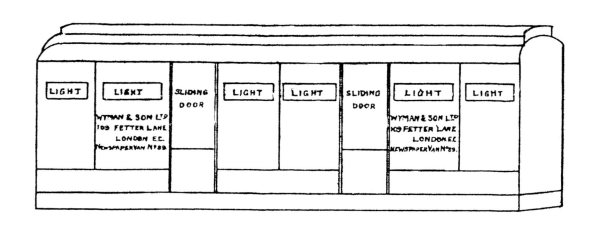

LENGTH OF VANS = 45'.0"

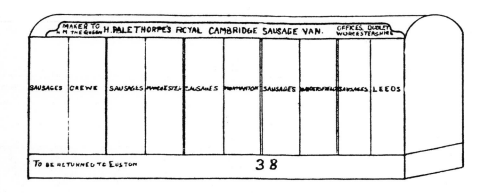

SAUSAGES	CREWE	SAUSAGES	WORCESTER	SAUSAGES	NORTHAMPTON	SAUSAGES	HUDDERSFIELD	SAUSAGES	LEEDS

MAKER TO H.M. THE QUEEN H.PALETHORPE'S ROYAL CAMBRIDGE SAUSAGE VAN. OFFICES DUDLEY WORCESTERSHIRE

To be returned to Euston 38

LENGTH OF TRUCK = 30'.1"

FOR PARCEL TRAFFIC PRYCE JONES LTD. NEWTOWN TO EUSTON

SHREWSBURY STAFFORD FOR NORTH	STAFFORD TRENT TAMWORTH	PARCELS BLETCHLEY NORTHAMPTON WILLESDEN	EUSTON EUSTON	EUSTON PARCELS POST EUSTON PARCELS POST

To be returned to Euston. 49

LENGTH OF TRUCK = 30'.1".

FOR PARCEL TRAFFIC PRYCE JONES LTD. NEWTOWN TO EUSTON

STAFFORD FOR NORTH SHREWSBURY	TAMWORTH STAFFORD TRENT	WILLESDEN PARCELS BLETCHLEY NORTHAMPTON	EUSTON EUSTON	EUSTON PARCELS POST EUSTON PARCELS POST

To be returned to Euston 57

LENGTH OF TRUCK = 30'.1"

Sundry Details

The 2'3" long destination boards, which fitted into brackets mounted above the windows, were white with black letters. Despite an article in the 1908 *Railway Magazine*, which specifies the converse, the WCJS were similar, except that those used on the earliest dining saloons of 1892-4 were painted to match the lake cantrail, and were lettered in gold. The 6'6" long roof-mounted detachable destination boards introduced in 1911 were ultramarine blue with cast-iron white painted letters screwed to the 8" deep boards. However, from 1897 certain vehicles carried permanently mounted roof boards, the length of which varied to suit the lettering. Examples of boards carried in 1909 by the 11.15am Euston to Bangor and Llandudno, and corresponding up working, were:

(20'4" long) NORTH WALES EXPRESS EUSTON & LLANDUDNO

(24' long)   NORTH WALES EXPRESS EUSTON BANGOR & PWLLHELI

(24' long)   NORTH WALES EXPRESS EUSTON BANGOR & PORTHMADOC

All the lettering on the 8" deep boards was rendered in 5" capitals. A variant used on the 'Sunny South Express' employed lettering 4½" high except for the initial letter of each word which was 5":-

LIVERPOOL (L&NWR) BRIGHTON & EASTBOURNE

Other portions of the train carried roof boards with MANCHESTER or BIRMINGHAM in place of LIVERPOOL.

The 'Outer Circle' stock of 1890-7 also carried roof boards, about 16ft long and narrower than those on main-line carriages, with the legend 'BROAD STREET, WILLESDEN, KENSINGTON & MANSION HOUSE. CHANGE AT WILLESDEN FOR MAIN LINE'. They also had small boards on the sides, about 3ft long, above the windows, but instead of showing a destination they were lettered 'LONDON & NORTH WESTERN TRAIN'. These were in the ordinary LNWR colours of white with black letters.

A number of details found on the solebars were prominent. A white-painted cast-iron letter 'A' 3" high was fixed near each vacuum cylinder (one nearly central before 1900 and one for each bogie on carriages built thereafter), to indicate the position of the vacuum brake; the release cock was operated by a small lever working in a quadrant with the letter 'A' fixed to the solebar next to it. A similar letter 'S' indicated the position of the steam-heat water-trap, while an arrow fixed about 1' away from the centre line of the coach denoted the release cock for the Westinghouse brake on dual-fitted vehicles.

Until 1914 a small plate 5½" × 4½" was fixed to the solebar at the right-hand end of the frame giving the dimensions of the vehicle. The plate was painted the same colour as the solebar with the 1" lettering and outer border picked out in white. From 1914 this plate was moved to the end of the carriage, and was painted grey with white letters on 9' wide stock and brown with white letters on narrower vehicles. At the same time the tare weight expressed in tons (for example, '29') was fixed in 3" white-painted cast-iron letters. Another small plate, 4" × 4½", was painted brown with red figures 1¼" high and indicated the seating capacity; for example, 'Seats/12/24' meant that the vehicle had accommodation for 12 first- and 24 third-class passengers. The LMS replaced the dimension plates by its own pattern but left the seating plates unaltered. From 1913 onwards a brown circular plate 3⅝" in diameter with a white letter 'R' on it 2" high was fixed on each side of the ends of 9' wide carriages fitted with the new pattern of steam regulator. All these details are shown in Fig.48. After 1914 another small plate was fitted to the headstock adjacent to the steam-heating case; this was 4½" × 4" with the words 'CLOSE

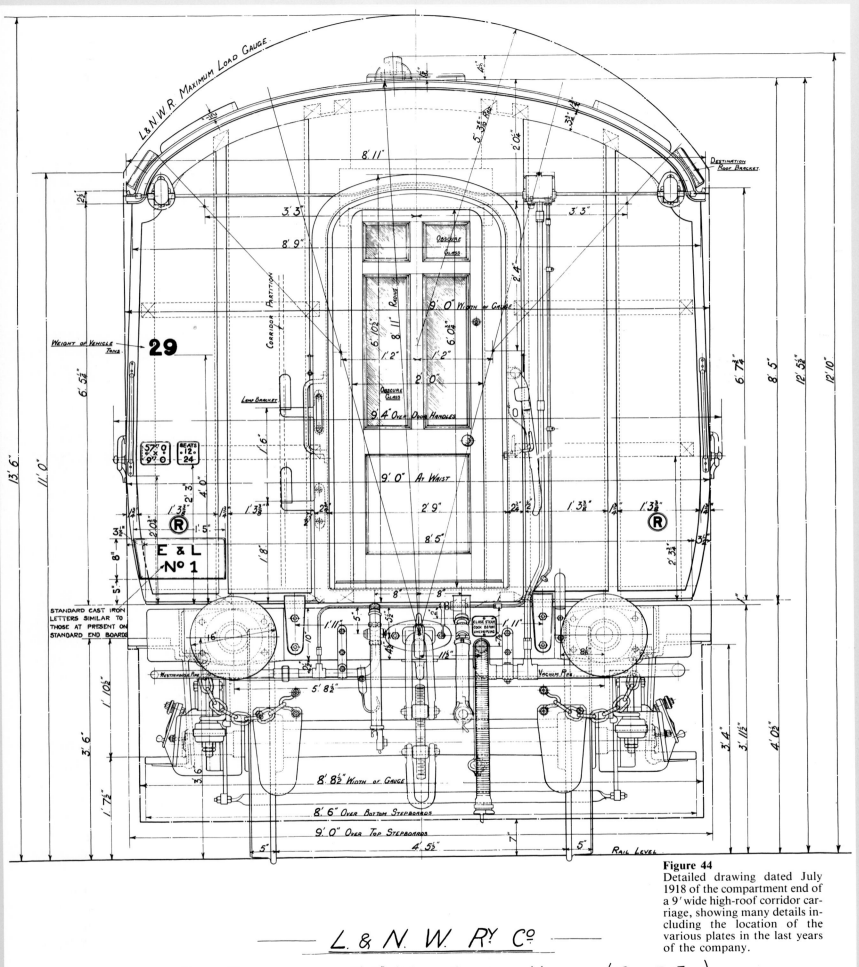

Figure 44
Detailed drawing dated July 1918 of the compartment end of a 9′ wide high-roof corridor carriage, showing many details including the location of the various plates in the last years of the company.

STEAM/COCK BEFORE/UNCOUPLING' in ½″ letters. At about the same time, a similar plate 9″×4½″ was fitted to the solebars of carriage trucks to specify the load capacity, and was in the form 'TO CARRY/5 TONS'. All these plates had a narrow raised border which was painted white. In the case of the large number of vehicles which were marshalled into semi-permanent set trains, an allocation board was provided at the outer ends of the set. It was located just above the headstock, and in the case of non-corridor stock extended right across the carriage. Examples are 'LIVERPOOL DISTRICT NO. 4' and 'CHESTER & HOLYHEAD NO. 9'. The white letters (including ampersands) were 1½″ high, with 2″ initials and 2¼″ figures. Corridor carriages had a shorter and deeper board, 17″×8″, mounted on the left-hand side of the gangway with two lines of white lettering, for example, 'INTER CORRIDOR/SET NO. 13'.

Sidelamps were fitted to all guard's brake compartments and were painted red. They were mounted on the ogees of those vehicles which had them. The brake pipes of vehicles which were vacuum- or Westinghouse-piped, but not fitted, were also red. Otherwise the flexible hose was brown, with one or two black bands to indicate the length — longer hoses were used on corridor stock.

All passenger-rated vehicles carried lamp irons in the following positions:
Corridor Vehicles Two lamp irons on the headstock, one on each side, spaced 2′3″ from the centre line.
Non-Corridor Vehicles Two lamp irons on the headstock, one on each side, spaced 2′3″ from the centre line in the case of vehicles 9′ in body width, and 1′3″ in the case of vehicles 8′ and 8′6″ wide. From July 1912 an additional lamp iron was provided, normally located on the moulding to the right of the centre line and 1′7″ above the bottom of the body. Exceptions were fruit vans, where the iron was set 1′1″ up and 1′10″ from the centre line, and horseboxes and 16′ fish vans where the distance from the centre line was 1′3″.
Open Carriage Trucks Both fixed and dropside versions had two lamp irons mounted 2′6″ apart on the headstocks; on fixed side vehicles only, an additional lamp iron was fitted from 1912, placed near the top of the end of the side, on the right-hand side as viewed from each end.

In LMS days these arrangements were modified and sometimes additional irons were fitted.

Interiors and Upholstery

Only fragmentary details survive of the colours of upholstery used in the nineteenth century; most of the information has been gathered from references in the locomotive committee minutes. In February 1860 it was ordered that cushions were to be fitted to second-class seats, and it was noted that for the last three or four years all new second-class carriages had been equipped with stuffed cushions and backs. In 1868 Mr Bore proposed that red Morocco leather should be used for trimming first-class compartments instead of American cloth, but this practice was quickly dropped and in the following year it was specified that blue cloth should be employed in the first class while the seconds were to be finished in brown and yellow striped rep (rep is a fabric with a corded surface, used in upholstery). At this stage third-class carriages were, of course, untrimmed. A pile carpet rug was provided on the floor in the firsts, but in smoking compartments coconut matting was used. The inferior classes had to make do with bare boards, perhaps until as late as 1900 when Greenwich inlaid lino was introduced.

In February 1873 it was ordered that first-class carriages should be fitted with spring blinds (which had previously been specified in 1869 but quickly countermanded). December 1874 saw the instruction for new second-class carriages to be fitted with superior stuffed seats, backs and elbows, with carpets or rugs on the floor, and window blinds, racks and hat straps. At the same time it was ordered that seats in the third class should be padded and covered in brown leather, but without back stuffing. In June 1875 came an instruc-

117

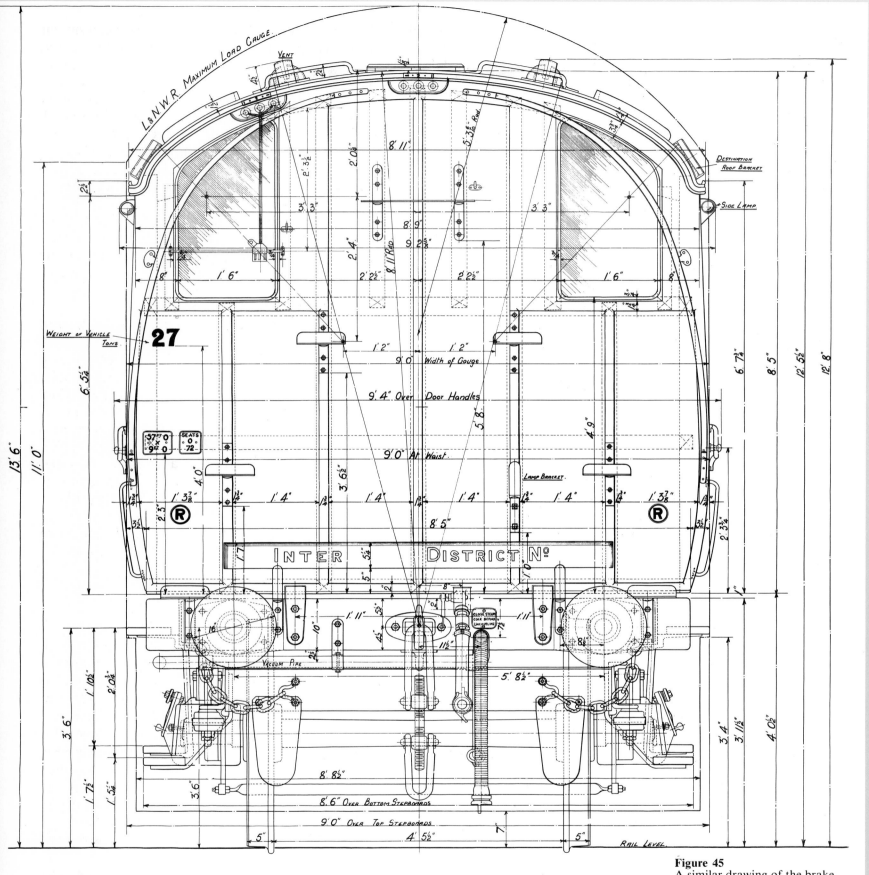

Figure 45
A similar drawing of the brake end of a 9′ wide non-corridor vehicle. This drawing dates from 1920.

L. & N. W. Rʸ Cᵒ

END ELEVATION OF 9′ 0″ WIDE NON-CORRIDOR VEHICLE. (BRAKE END)

WOLVERTON.   SCALE 1½″ = 1 FOOT.   29. 3. 20.

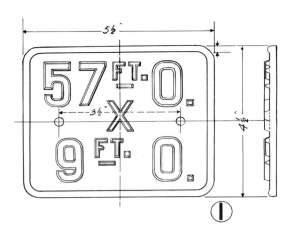

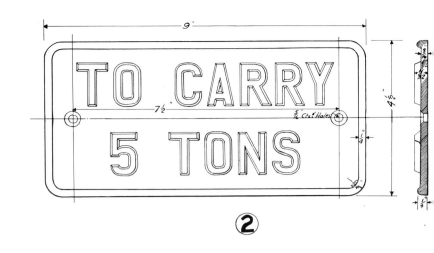

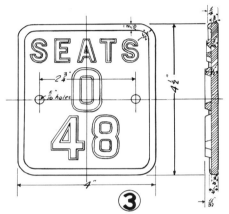

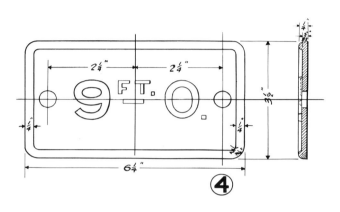

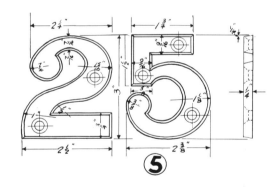

Nº of Drawing	Name of Plate	Explanation	Where Situated	Colour Painted
1	Dimension Plate	Showing Length and Width	On End of Body	9'0. Grey Plate White Letters 8'6 Brown Plate 8'0 White Letters
2	Tonnage Plate	Carrying Capacity in Tons	Solebar	
3	Seating Accommodation	0 Firsts 48 Thirds	On End of Body	Brown Plate Red Letters
4	Bogie Wheelbase Indicator Plate		On Bogie Solebar	
5	Weight	Weight of Vehicle To the Nearest Ton	On End of Body	White
6	Steam Cock Notice	Instructions for closing Steam Cock of Heating Apparatus	Headstock	Black Plate White Letters
7	Steam Regulators	Fitted with Steam Regulators New Pattern	On End of Body	Brown Plate White Letters
8	Slip Release	Denotes Slip Coach & Slip Release	On Headstock	Red
9	S	Chain for Steam Trap of Heating Apparatus	On Solebar	White
10	Arrow	Release for Westinghouse Brake	"	"
11	A	Release for Vacuum Brake	"	"

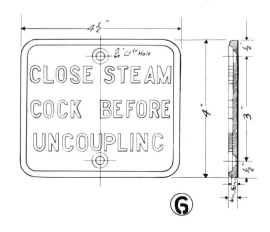

Figure 46
Large-scale details of the various plates and symbols applied to carriages.

119

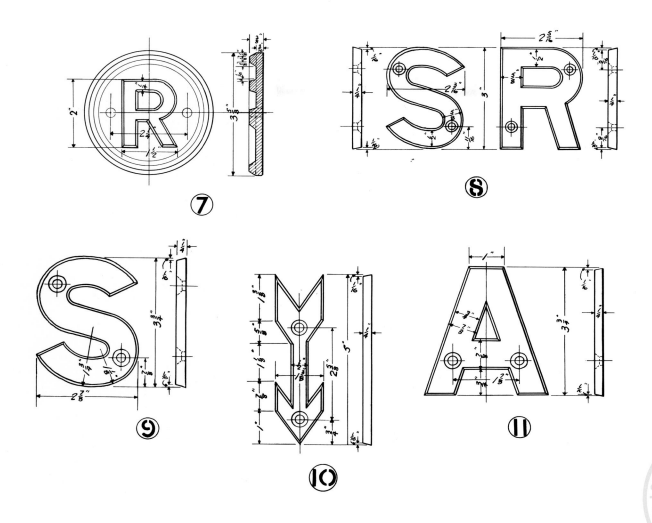

tion to fit moveable arm rests in the first-class compartments of some of the best composite carriages.

The order was given in October 1876 for padded seats and trimming to be fitted to all outstanding second- and third-class compartments over the subsequent two years. Centre arm rests were extended to WCJS second-class compartments in May 1879, while at the same time WCJS thirds were upgraded with blinds and high stuffed seat backs.

During the nineteenth century frequent changes were made to the compartment designations of many carriages, with the result that firsts could change to seconds, composites or thirds, and back again (with correspondingly frequent changes in the vehicle's number). Whether these changes involved the refurbishment of the upholstery to match the new status is not known, but it is thought to be unlikely, although centre arm rests may well have been removed on down-grading. On the other hand, when the upholstery required renewal (every five to eight years) it would doubtless have been replaced by that appropriate to the new class designation.

There is general agreement that the colour of the upholstery in first-class compartments immediately prior to the grouping was a floral-patterned lovat green. This applied to both the LNWR and the WCJS, and as far as can be determined green had always been the normal WCJS colour. The original corridor carriages of 1893 had 'green and silver moquette' — presumably 'silver' refers to white wool — but contemporary accounts state that the 1897 WCJS set trains were upholstered in a crushed strawberry colour while the 1913 WCJS vehicles were crimson with dark red leather trimmings. Nevertheless, the weight of evidence suggests that before the war the normal colour for LNWR first-class upholstery

Plate 111
LNWR rug from a first-class
compartment, showing the
elaborately woven coat of arms.
Photo c.1921 by J.P.Richards.

was blue. The use of blue upholstery was never completely abandoned, for it was certainly used on the Oerlikon electric stock, and blue moquette, carpets and curtain cloth were being purchased in 1920. At this distance in time, it is not possible to reconcile all the pieces of evidence, but the most likely explanation is that a change was made from blue to green in 1908 for LNWR new construction but that existing vehicles continued to be refurbished in blue.

The lower part of first-class compartment doors and the upper part of the arm rests were covered in red leather, and some smoking compartments in suburban carriages were upholstered entirely in red leather.

There is also general agreement that the second class was dark red, which may either have been plain or patterned with black. In the last century the third class seems to have been green, but from about 1897 changed to a greenish-yellow or yellowish-brown with black tracery; when second class was abolished in 1912 the thirds became dark red. However, the third class was of a rougher material and, in later years at least, included a black floral pattern in the design. Again, the WCJS appears to have been different, as the thirds in the 1897 stock were brown and black rep, and in the 1909 stock were crimson and black patterned velvet. It is not now possible to establish precise details of these changes, and in any case older designs would have remained in use for some years until refurbishment of the upholstery became necessary.

A number of Wolverton drawings prepared late in 1908 cover the finishing of the first-, second- and third-class compartments according to the 'new design'. Blenheim or Saladin moquette (of unstated colour) was specified for the first class, crimson and black moquette for the seconds, and brown and gold rep for the thirds. It is thought that the brown and gold rep design was in use only until 1912. In July 1920 it was noted that moquette had risen in price from 6s 4d per yard pre-war to 33s 9d, and a new design would reduce the price by 2s 8d per yard, saving £2266 per annum on the total requirement of 17000 yards.

121

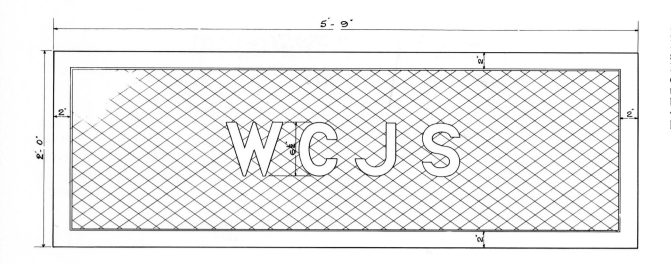

The only official records of upholstery which survive relate to an order placed on 20th October 1920 for 3100 yards of black and crimson rep, 2000 yards of blue moquette, 500 yards of brown Tammy and 500 yards of black velveteen. The use to which the last two materials were put is unclear, particularly the velveteen which is not a heavy duty material and would hardly be suitable for upholstery. Possibly they were used for staff uniforms. A little later, an order was placed for blue, fawn and green curtain cloth with the LNWR or WCJS monogram.

First-class compartments were supplied with a patterned rug, woven with the LNWR or WCJS coat of arms as appropriate, and in either dark and light blue or green to match the upholstery. In the years immediately before the grouping, these were supplied by Maple & Co in various sizes, 7'6", 6'10", 6'7" and 5'9" long by 2'6" wide to suit different

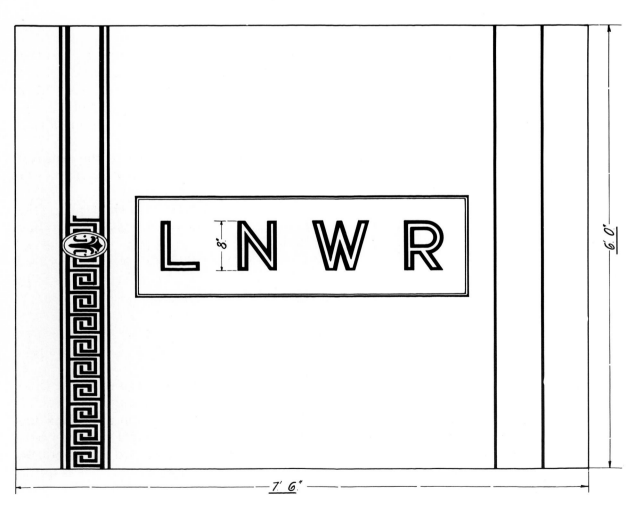

122

compartments, different orders specifying the LNWR 'medallion' and the LNWR 'monogram'. The same supplier also delivered large quantities of carpet, typical orders calling for crimson pile carpet (both with and without a black border), special red Wilton carpet, special green Wilton carpet, and green pile bordered carpet. The normal floor covering for third-class compartments was figured Kork linoleum, but during the first war a proprietary fireproof material known as Decolite was extensively used. This was also laid in lavatory compartments, brake vans, parcels and fish vans, as well as in other vehicles. The woodwork in the first class was generally walnut with sycamore panels, while in the third class mahogany or Burma teak was used. Both classes had the usual sepia photographs on the partitions above seats, and in the first class mirrors and white anti-maccassars were fitted.

Fairly extensive details survive of the furnishings of dining and sleeping saloons, but as they have been described elsewhere it is not necessary to repeat them there. For further information the books mentioned in the bibliography should be consulted.

The interiors of covered carriage trucks, brake, milk, parcels and post office vans were painted pea green, and the latter had the sorting tables covered in green baize. Every carriage door had a small enamelled plate fixed on the inside near the top giving the number of the carriage in black numerals on a white ground, while the compartment class was also indicated in yellow numerals positioned just below the window, thus: '1st', '2nd' or '3rd', with the word 'SMOKING' if appropriate.

Plate 112 *(G.H.Platt collection)* A bird's eye view of Wolverton Gravel Sidings in 1908 shows white roofs in abundance on newly overhauled carriages, although a number are sooty grey. On the original print it is possible to distinguish a 50' brake-composite of D216 with roof boards lettered 'London Euston, Barrow and Whitehaven'.

Plate 113 *National Railway Museum (Crown Copyright)* Vehicles withdrawn from revenue service often found a further lease of life as departmental stock. This photograph is particularly interesting, as it shows Nos. 2149A and 2150A in use as riding vans with the Crewe Breakdown train. These had started life as two of the four infamous WCJS 34′ sleeping saloons of 1881 — their complicated career is described in *A Register of West Coast Joint Stock*. The vehicles are painted in 'horsebox brown' without any lining but with standard yellow block lettering — note the smaller size of the 'A', which denoted a vehicle which was already on the supplementary list at the time of the 1910 renumbering. The ultimate fate of these vehicles is obscure, but they probably survived for some years after the grouping although they never received LMS numbers or insignia. In the background is the unique 40′ Tool van which was specially built for this train.

Paint Specifications

The following is an amalgam of a number of paint specifications, both published and unpublished, all of which are in general agreement but which sometimes give additional details:-

Preparation: 8 coats of priming, filling etc.

Above Waist

Undercoats: 2 coats white lead colour, made up as follows in the paint mixer:

White lead	$\frac{3}{4}$ cwt
Ultramarine Blue	$\frac{3}{4}$ lb
Linseed Oil	$\frac{1}{2}$ gallon
White Spirits	1 gallon
Paste Dryers	7 lb

3rd Coat: Flake White, ground in the paint mill as follows:

Dry White lead	14 lb
Ultramarine Blue	2 oz
Sugar of Lead	$1\frac{3}{4}$ lb
Linseed Oil	2 pints
White Spirits	2 pints

4th Coat: Varnish White, made up as follows:

Flake White (as above)	10 lb
Body Varnish	6 pints
White Spirits	1 gill

Below Waist

1st Coat: Lead Colour (afterwards stop and face with pumice stone).

2nd Coat: Body Brown, ground in the paint mill as follows:

Drop Black	10 lb
Indian Red	$9\frac{1}{2}$ lb
Liquid Dryers	2 lb
Sugar of Lead	1 lb
Linseed Oil	6 pints

3rd Coat: Carmine Lake, ground in the paint mill as follows:

Lake Powder	2 lb
Sugar of Lead	8 oz
Linseed Oil	3 pints

After grinding, 1 pint of Liquid Driers and ½ pint White Spirit added.

4th Coat: Varnish Colour, made up as follows:

Carmine Lake (as above)   3 lb
Varnish   2 pints

After lining and lettering has been carried out, 4 coats of varnish to be applied. All paint to be applied at the rate of not more than one coat per day, and two days to be allowed between each coat of varnish. The varnish to contain no gold size.

In November 1922, on the eve of the grouping, the LNWR invited tenders for the supply of the following paints, intended to cover one year's usage, to the carriage department at Wolverton:

200 cwt   zinc white
 30 cwt   drop black
  2 cwt   ultramarine blue
  5 cwt   yellow ochre
  3 cwt   chrome lemon
  1 cwt   chrome orange
 18 cwt   indian red
  8 cwt   vermilion substitute
  ½ cwt   burnt sienna
  ½ cwt   burnt turkey umber
  2 cwt   carmine lake (to consist of cochineal mordanted on
             to alumina)
 28 lb   gold powder (finely powered alloy of copper,
             aluminium and zinc)

The use to which each paint was put is mostly obvious, but the burnt sienna and burnt turkey umber were mixed with varnish for interior staining. The requirement for such a large quantity of vermilion is less clear — apart from details such as train alarm chains and guard's brake valves, this colour did not feature in any paint specification, and may have been used mainly for painting machinery in the works.

Plate 114 *National Railway Museum (Crown Copyright)*
10-ton open goods wagon No. 50195 to D84 lettered for use as a coal wagon. This was the last standard open wagon design and was first introduced in 1904, although quantity production did not begin until 1907. 15857 examples passed to the LMS, including some built on government account in the war.

7

GOODS ROLLING STOCK

by **Philip Millard**

Only fragmentary details of the paint schemes of goods rolling stock in the early years survive; according to Sir Francis Head, writing in 1849, the colour of cattle and merchandise wagons at that time was usually blue, while sheep wagons were green. Thereafter no documentary evidence appears until 1881, but it is almost certain that at that date goods wagons and vans had been painted a light or medium grey colour for many years previously, probably from the late 1850s. The running gear and buffer heads were painted black, and goods vans had white roofs when new. This basic colour scheme continued until the grouping, with occasional variations. About the turn of the century the outside framing of vans, including brake vans, was often very dark grey or even black in colour, contrasting quite sharply with the lighter grey of the planking. From about 1908 onwards the roofs of ordinary covered vans were often painted grey also, but refrigerator, banana, fruit and other 'special' vans retained white roofs.

Photographs taken at Earlestown works about 1900 show open wagons which appear very dark in colour; this appears to be dark grey paint but may possibly be creosote. A minute of March 1885 called for 100 mineral and locomotive coal wagons to be treated with creosote, 100 with chloride of zinc and 100 with naptholine for comparative experimental purposes, but it appears that the experiment was not a great success although the use of creosote seems to have continued intermittently for the next ten or fifteen years.

There were a few other departures from the normal grey livery. The special cattle wagons

Plate 115   *National Railway Museum (Crown Copyright)* 7-ton open goods wagon No. 38909 of Diagram 2 in 1909 in the short-lived 'hybrid' lettering style with both diamonds and large 'LNWR' lettering. Vast quantities of these wagons were constructed between 1870 and 1894, and no less than 13826 were running in 1902, although thereafter their numbers declined as they were replaced by more modern designs. 9100 remained at the end of 1909 and 324 were handed over to the LMS.

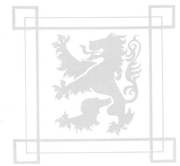

Plate 116 *(G.H.Platt collection)*

A ballast train headed by No. 2157 UNICORN at Watford in 1894-5. The wagon behind the tender is one of the earliest examples of Diagram 4 with 36″ sides, and is lettered 'COAL WAGON' in about 7″ letters on the second plank. The next three wagons are 9″ side vehicles to D1.

of types 23-6 were painted in the brown/lake colour used for non-passenger coaching stock, and lined out in a simplified style. Refrigerator vans were painted white from their introduction in 1886; originally only the horizontal planking was white, all the framing around the doors, corner posts, end pillars, curb and cant rails being black. Solebars and headstocks were also black in this style. Early in the present century this scheme was simplified; solebars, headstocks and the curb rail or capping strip along the bottom of the bodyside were now painted the standard grey, with all the remainder of the body white. The same livery applied to the 75 butter vans which were white from their introduction in 1899 until 1911, when they were demoted to the status of ventilated goods vans (Type 19) and painted in the ordinary grey livery. Another variant was that old wagons unfit for further mainline service were painted red and transferred to the service stock for internal use only, at the same time having the cypher Ø placed in front of their numbers.

Nevertheless, the overwhelming majority of goods wagons were a plain medium lead grey, the paint being mixed from black and white pigments in equal proportions and accordingly a little darker than LMS wagon grey. Doubtless the precise shade varied from time to time and was further modified by the effects of dirt and weathering. While there is no doubt that gunpowder vans were grey by about 1912, they were probably red at some previous time, as contemporary models by Bassett-Lowke (which usually took great trouble to get the livery details of its models correct) are all painted in this colour. There were only 26 of these vehicles at the most.

The familiar diamond marks are of very ancient origin, being derived from the Egyptian diamond of the GJR, when wagons for destinations on the Liverpool & Manchester line were marked with a diamond. At that time, however, it was a hollow figure rather than the solid one of later years, and in this form it was in use, presumably as an identity rather than a destination mark, by the early 1850s, as it is shown in one of the illustrations of a Southern Division wagon in D.K.Clark's *Railway Machinery*, Plate XLIII. Wagons allocated to the Chester & Holyhead section seem to have been adorned with the Prince of Wales feathers, but a minute of September 1860 ordered this practice to be discontinued.

The first official reference to the diamond marks occurs in a minute of April 1859, which refers to '. . . red diamond small coke wagons . . .', implying that other wagons were marked differently. Ten months later the general stores committee called for wagons to be 'lettered only L&NW and white diamond' — note the use of the singular. No photographs have been found with any marking like this, and from 1881 (or earlier) until 1908 the only markings on ordinary goods stock were two solid white diamonds, 11″ by 5½″ in size. Their exact positioning varied according to the position of framing, strapping

129

Plate 117 *National Railway Museum (Crown Copyright)*
Coke wagon No. 5005 of D31 was one of about 20 allocated to the carriage department and worked between Coventry Gas Works and Wolverton. The photograph was taken in 1906 before the introduction of the large LNWR lettering.

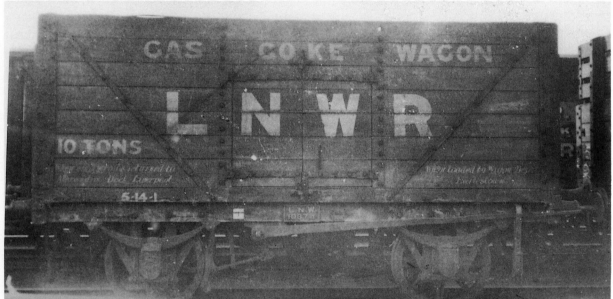

Plate 118 *(J.P.Richards)*
Another D31 coke wagon, No. 10374, allocated to the wagon department and photographed shortly before the grouping. The small italic lettering below the '10 TONS' legend reads 'When empty to be returned to Alexandra Dock, Liverpool' while that on the right reads 'When loaded to Wagon Dept. Earlestown'.

Plate 119 *National Railway Museum (Crown Copyright)*
10 ton loco coal wagon No. 45573 of D64 was photographed in 1910 and displays the 'hybrid' lettering style of the period. The word 'LOCO' is made from cast-iron letters and the wagon has been fitted with oil axleboxes and modern either-side brakes. There were roughly 3000 to this design in service during the present century.

and any other markings, and photographs have to be consulted for individual cases. A good selection is given in plates 166-172 of *L.N.W.R. Miscellany, Volume 1* and plates 94-102 of *ibid, Volume 2*.

Many, but not all, goods brake vans carried the name of the yard or goods depot to which they were allocated in 5″ letters on the bottom frame member of the body sides. A few vans were reserved for particular services, for example, Crewe and Carlisle, in which case this lettering was similarly displayed. Possibly, the practice of allocating specific brake vans to depots ceased during the war, and thereafter brake vans were regarded as 'common user'.

Wagons for various special purposes, or designed for particular traffics, carried additional lettering. Thus, a photograph taken in 1885 showing part of Crewe steam shed includes wagons marked:

LONDON & NORTH WESTERN

◆ RAILWAY ◆

COAL WAGON

in approximately 6″ letters. Locomotive coal wagons at this time had the word 'LOCO' in letters 16″ high in the centre of the side, flanked by a diamond on each side. For a period from 1885 loco coal wagons were usually coated with creosote instead of being painted, in which case the word 'LOCO' and the diamonds were of white-painted cast iron, screwed into position. The cast-iron letters were 12″ in height only. In 1902 a series of 60 steel loco coal wagons were constructed to Type 65, and on these the letters and symbols were embossed in the steel plate of the sides.

Plate 121   *National Railway Museum (Crown Copyright)*
18′ refrigerator van No. 54849 of D46A; some 225 of these were built in the 1909-22 period with further examples for the WCJS. The solebar, curb rail and ladder are grey; the words 'Refrigerator Van Return to Liverpool' appear too light in colour to be black, and may be red, but whether this was usual practice at the time cannot be determined. By 1920 all the lettering was certainly black.

Plate 122   *National Railway Museum (Crown Copyright)*
7-ton small class wagon No. 7960 to D39, one of fifty constructed in 1893 and photographed in 1909. All glass wagons seem to have been similarly lettered for return to St Helens.

132

Meat vans carried their designation and the service to which they were allocated in block letters arranged either side of the doors just below the roof, thus:-

MEAT	RETURN TO
VAN	CREWE

The wording 'REFRIGERATOR VAN' appeared on all vehicles of this description (in black letters on the white body) with the legend '*To be returned to LIVERPOOL*' immediately below. This was rendered in italic script at first, but became block characters from 1913.

It was also usual on wagons with 36″ sides to paint the maximum permitted load, for example, '7 TONS', in 6″ characters on each side on the top plank. This was ordered by a minute of April 1896 after complaints of damage due to overloading. The earliest style of this lettering was widely spaced with '7' to the left of the door and 'TONS' to the right, located above the diamond symbols. When the 'L N W R' lettering was adopted, the inscription, for example, '10 TONS', was placed near the left-hand end on the top plank, while from about 1921 'L N W R' was placed somewhat higher up on the vehicle side and the '10 TONS' designation moved to or repeated on the bottom plank at the right-hand end.

Traffic coal wagons of type 53 carried the inscription '8 TONS COAL WAGON' on the top plank in 6″ characters; from 1904 onwards many of these were reconstructed to carry 10 tons (type 54) in which case the inscription was adjusted accordingly. These wagons were fitted with bottom doors and in later years at least this was indicated by painting diagonal white stripes, some 3½″ wide and 12″ long on the top plank only, in such a way as to cover the diagonal iron strapping. A number of ordinary goods wagons without bottom doors were also allocated for coal traffic, in which case they also carried the inscription on the top plank.

The unique covered goods van No. 13389 of type 36 was marked '*To work between / CREWE AND CHESTER*' in small letters on the curb rail; the even larger van No. 14333 of type 37 carried a small board on the bottom right-hand corner of the bodyside

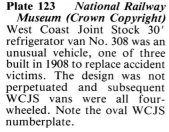

Plate 123 *National Railway Museum (Crown Copyright)* West Coast Joint Stock 30′ refrigerator van No. 308 was an unusual vehicle, one of three built in 1908 to replace accident victims. The design was not perpetuated and subsequent WCJS vans were all four-wheeled. Note the oval WCJS numberplate.

Plate 124 *National Railway Museum (Crown Copyright)*
West Cumberland District hopper coke wagon No. 25190 to D29, of which 131 were in service for most of the 1902-22 period. Hopper wagons to D44 allocated to the Cleator District were externally similar but without the coke raves; on these, the angle iron around the top edge, and the upper 3″ of the topmost plank, were painted white according to a 1909 photograph.

Plate 125 *National Railway Museum (Crown Copyright)*
16′ butter van No. 64769 was one of 75 built in 1899-1900 to D19. The date of the photograph is unknown, but probably about 1909. The original lettering style of these vans is unknown — it is unlikely that they carried the large LNWR lettering from new as this was not introduced on grey wagons until 1908. In 1911 these vans were reclassified as ordinary goods vans and thereafter carried the normal grey livery.

Plate 126 *National Railway Museum (Crown Copyright)*
This unique 40′ bogie tool van was specially built in 1914 for the Crewe breakdown train. The complete train is depicted in Plate 113.

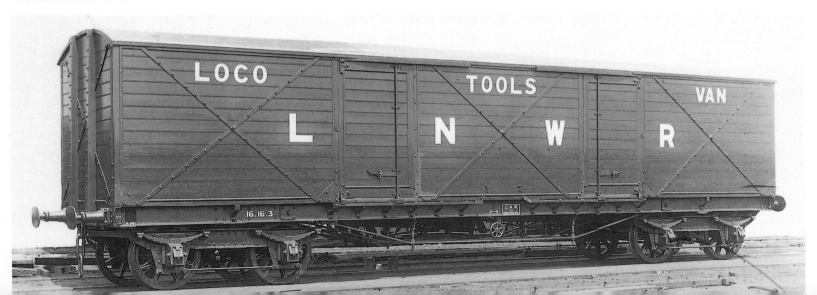

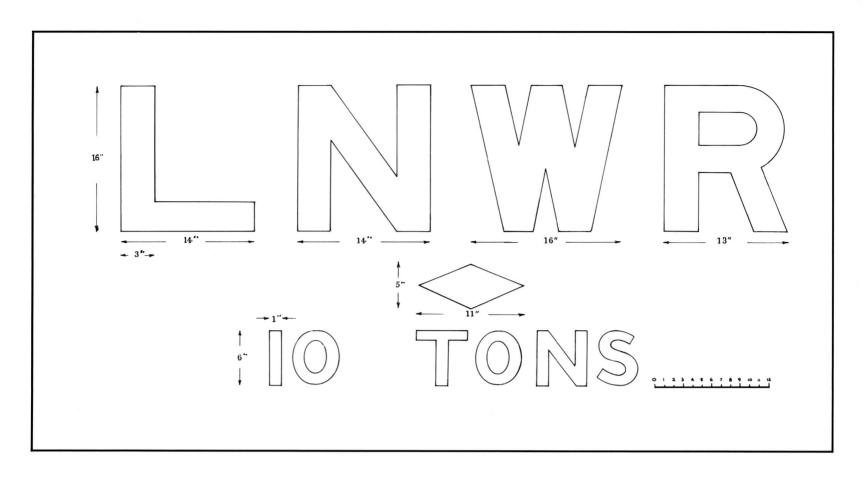

Figure 49 *(B.C.Lane)*
LNWR standard wagon lettering.

which carried the inscription *'To work between Warrington and Crewe'*. Both of these vans were probably allocated to parcels traffic and were built experimentally in 1903.

Towards the end of 1907 moves were made to display the company's initials on goods stock, as had already been done by most other railways, and a minute of March 1908 called for new wagons and those going through works to be lettered 'L & N W R', though when the instruction was actually put into effect the ampersand was omitted. The diamond symbols were retained for a few years more, being apparently discontinued soon after A.F.Trevithick took over as wagon superintendent at Earlestown in 1910. An Earlestown photograph with the paint date 6/10 carries the diamonds, whereas another dated 10/11 does not. However, when older vehicles which had originally carried the diamond markings were repainted at outstations, it was by no means unusual to paint them on again. One recorded example of a ballast wagon repainted in 1924 in LMS grey retained the 'SD' lettering and white diamonds, and it is clear that the diamond markings were still to be seen well after the grouping.

The letters adopted in 1908 were 16″ high on ordinary open wagons but on low-sided wagons and special vehicles they had to be reduced to fit the space available. Thus, on single-plank wagons the letters were 13″ high, on glass wagons 9″ and on bolster wagons, timber wagons and similar vehicles, where the letters were on the solebars, they were reduced to 6″.

A minute of August 1882 called for the number of the wagon to be painted on the ends in the same manner as on the Caledonian Railway. The number was painted in 4″ characters in the centre of the top plank, but 3″ characters were used on timber trucks and bolster wagons. Before that the number was to be found only on the cast-iron plate fitted to the solebar near the centre of the wagon (and that on one side only until about 1878). These ownership/numberplates were rectangular, 13″ × 6½″, bearing the initials 'L.N.W.' (with full points) and the wagon number beneath it in 2″ characters. These plates were painted black, the raised lettering and outer border being picked out in white. Brake vans were numbered in a separate series to revenue-earning stock, and here the vehicle's number

135

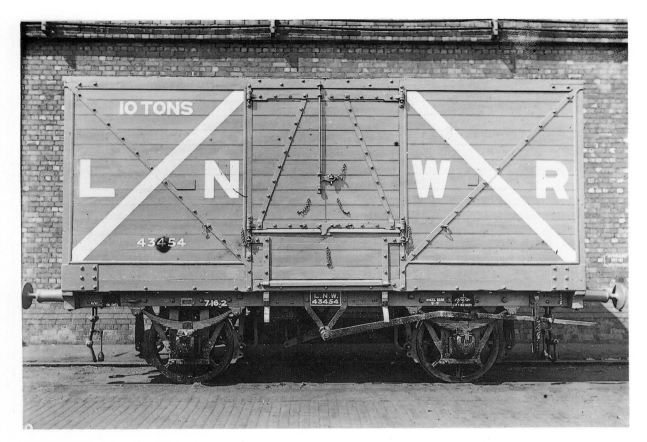

Plate 127 *National Railway Museum (Crown Copyright)*
10-ton goods van No. 43454 was a late example of the numerous D88 vans and was photographed in 1921. The two white stripes indicated that the vehicle is fully fitted — piped vehicles displayed one stripe only. The number is painted on the side as well as shown on the numberplate. This is the first recorded example of this practice, which does not seem to have become general until after the grouping.

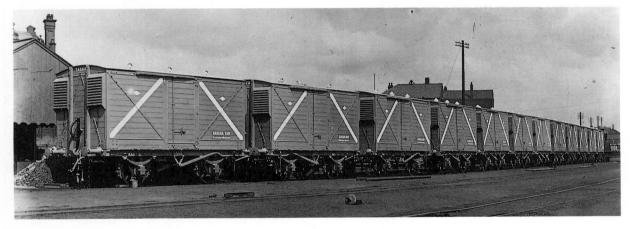

Plate 128 *National Railway Museum (Crown Copyright)*
A train of 18′ fruit vans to D95, of which 200 were turned out in 1905. All appear to have been lettered for banana traffic. The two stripes indicate that the vehicles are fully fitted and the photo shows the pre-1908 lettering style with diamonds rather than large 'LNWR' letters. The label board on the side reads 'BANANA VAN To be returned to Manchester'. These vans were fitted with steam heating, which was by no means universal for passenger stock at this date. Another 325 were built in the 1911-13 period, and yet another 100 to D95A in 1922-3.

was followed by a B suffix; the letter 'B' was $\frac{3}{4}$″ high in contrast to the 2″ of the numerals.

Official photographs of goods stock, particularly vans, occasionally show the number painted on the side in various positions, without any consistency, and most are thought to be experimental. Some photographs taken in the 1920s show wagons with numbers painted low down on the left-hand side. These numbers were added in early LMS days, often before any other repainting and before renumbering.

In 1896 the inspector of Irish cattle traffic drew attention to the difficulties in ascertaining the numbers of cattle trucks owing to the numbers being on the ends of the vehicles only, and it was ordered that as cattle wagons entered the works for repairs their numbers should be painted on the sides also. The numbers were painted in $3\frac{1}{2}$″ characters above the right-hand diamond but this practice seems to have been discontinued again during the First World War. Until about 1909 small letters 'P.F' were placed after the number to indicate pipe-fitted vehicles, but this was then discontinued. The words 'SMALL', 'MEDIUM' or 'LARGE' as appropriate were painted on the top rail at the right-hand end, immediately below the roof, although 'SMALL' cattle wagons were uncommon at the turn of the century and virtually extinct by 1914.

Figure 50 *(J.P.Richards)*
A selection of LNWR wagon plates.

L.N.W. 64972	L.N.W. 13591
L.N.W. 460	L.N.W. 4853
L & N W. 1683 BALLAST	L & N W. 783 BALLAST
L.N.W. 740 B	L.N.W. 1400 B
	L.N.W. 1543 B

137

Plate 129 *(G.H.Platt collection)*

No. 52356 is one of the postwar examples of refrigerator vans to D95A and shows the then usual arrangement of lettering. This van is to be returned to Garston.

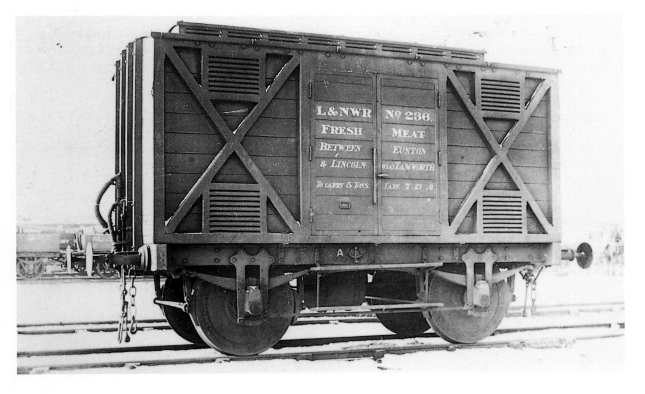

Plate 130 *(G.H.Platt collection)*

Meat van No. 236 appears to have a Great Northern Railway body mounted on an LNWR 16′ carriage truck underframe! No records relating to these vans have been located, and thus how many there were and when they were built is unknown. However, the serif lettering style probably gives a clue to the general arrangement of lettering on these and similar vehicles in the pre-1890 period, although the photograph was almost certainly taken around 1900.

The tare weight of each wagon was painted on the left-hand end of the solebar, usually on the bottom edge, in 3″ figures (2½″ on timber and bolster wagons), but after 1912 it was moved up on to the curb rail or bottom plank of the bodyside.

Other markings were used to indicate special purposes or variations from standard. Ordinary goods vans fitted with continuous brakes (of which many were constructed from 1905 onwards) had a 6″ wide diagonal stripe across each end panel of the side, and those with through pipes had the stripe at the left-hand end only. However, these stripes were not applied to banana, meat or fruit vans, which were reserved for those commodities, nor to refrigerator vans. Insulated vans had a 2′ diameter circle in white on the lower right-hand corner of each side. The brake pipes on wagons and vans which were fitted with through pipes (as opposed to full vacuum brake gear) were painted red, a standard practice on all railways. This was particularly relevant to cattle wagons, all of which constructed from December 1898 were required to have through pipes and screw couplings, while many ordinary goods vans built in the present century were similarly equipped.

Ballast wagons were also lettered differently from the traffic (or revenue-earning) stock. For day-to-day purposes ballast wagons came under the control of the civil engineer, although the wagon department was responsible for their repair and renewal. For this reason each wagon carried two different numbers; the solebar plate carried the serial number of the wagon allocated by the wagon department at Earlestown in the form 'L&NW./1713/BALLAST' and this number could range from 1 to about 2100. This solebar plate was 15″×7″ or somewhat larger than the normal wagon plate; the wagon number was rendered in 2″ figures, the other lettering being 1½″ in height. In addition, another plate was fixed centrally to the bottom plank at one end only giving the number of the wagon and its district allocation in the engineering department list; this plate was also 15″×7″ and was of the form 'L&NWR C^{o}/BALLAST/140 WD.' Until 1889 there were only five engineering districts, namely the Northern, Southern, Holyhead, Carlisle and the 'Engineering Stores' districts, but in that year a reorganisation took place which increased the number to nine, as follows:

SD   Southern Division (Watford)
RD   Rugby Division
CD   Central Division (Crewe)
BD   Birmingham and Walsall Division
ED   Eastern Division (Manchester)
WD   Western Division (Liverpool)

Plate 131   *(J.P.Richards)*
16′ meat van No. 62014 to D45 soon after the grouping — the paint date is 1/23. It is lettered for Hawick and London traffic (Hawick being on the North British Railway which ruled out the use of West Coast Joint Stock). All the others seem to have been allocated as well, other legends being 'RETURN TO CREWE' and 'RETURN TO LIVERPOOL'. The diamond marks were originally displayed on the second plank from the bottom, and the '6 TONS' marking is a post-1908 innovation.

139

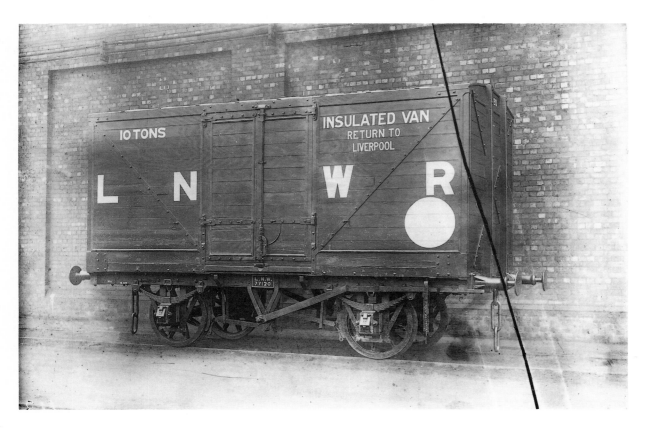

Plate 132 *National Railway Museum (Crown Copyright)* 18′ goods van No. 77120 of D88A in 1918 with the 24″ diameter white circle which indicates that it is an insulated van. It may have been the first to carry this marking.

Plate 133 *National Railway Museum (Crown Copyright)* Cattle box No. 72332 was one of ten built in 1902 and was described in the diagram book as 'Cattle Wagon with compartment for man'. Diagrams 23-26 covered several varieties of these cattle boxes with drover's compartments, and although they were the responsibility of Earlestown works they were finished in the 'quick brown' colour used for horseboxes and other non-passenger coaching stock, and were lined out in yellow. From about 1908 the legend '6 TONS' appeared on the bottom plank at the left-hand end on each side.

ND Northern Division (Lancaster)
NWD North Wales Division (Bangor)
SWD South Wales Division (Abergavenny)

Ballast wagons were also used at engine sheds for the removal of ashes and for bringing sand from the sand pits. In addition, many ballast wagons were, in later years at least, allocated to the engineer at Crewe for new works and major relaying projects. It is almost certain that this applies only to the post-1913 period as no reference to this central allocation has been found in the records, which in any case are woefully inadequate after this date. In February 1913 it was ordered that 400 traffic department wagons should be transferred to the engineering department for ballasting and it would appear that these are the vehicles involved. According to contemporary observations these wagons were lettered 'PWD' in 12″ letters on the sides and had the word 'CREWE' in 5″ letters painted on the top plank at the end in the same position where an ordinary wagon displayed its number. In this case there was no cast plate on the end, nor did the 'PWD' wagons ever display the two white diamonds, as they had been discontinued in 1911. In the case of ballast wagons allocated to the districts, cast-iron white-painted letters 9″ high were fixed to the top plank at one end of the wagon only (the same end as the cast plate, of course) indicating the district to which they were attached. In addition, the same letters were painted in either 12″ or 15″ characters spaced 30″ apart centrally on the side of the wagon. The smaller 12″ letters may have been a wartime economy measure. In 1920 most, but not all, ballast wagons had these large letters. Even on the eve of the grouping a large proportion carried the usual two diamonds on the sides; they were located on the top plank with their centres 2′6″ from the adjacent inner iron strapping, and hence were not exactly central in the space nor directly above the axleboxes, but somewhat closed in towards the centre of the wagon.

A minute of 1860 called for these wagons to be lettered 'BALLAST' 'in large letters' but the style described above was in use by 1895 at the latest. A photograph taken in the 1880s shows a Holyhead District wagon with the letters 'H.D' (with single full point) 6″ high placed centrally on the side between the two diamonds; thus the large letters were probably introduced in 1889 when the nine districts were formed. In later years at least, wagons allocated to the Central Division could be lettered either '◆ C D ◆' or with only one diamond, thus 'C ◆ D'. It is not known if this represented any distinction in usage.

Plate 134 *National Railway Museum (Crown Copyright)* The LNWR maintained a fleet of 270 beer vans of which No. 23473 of D15 is an example. The date is December 1907 and both diamonds and 'LNWR' letters are displayed.

141

Plate 135 *National Railway Museum (Crown Copyright)* No. 31235 was a bulk grain van, one of 25 converted in November 1920 from beer vans to cater for a grain contract with the Liverpool Grain Storage & Transit Co. The contract ceased in 1927.

Plate 136 *National Railway Museum (Crown Copyright)* Large cattle wagon No. 15483 in October 1909; apart from the lettering the wood is unpainted. It is not clear whether this was normal practice; lead-based paints could injure animals which licked them, but it is unlikely that this danger was appreciated at this time, and other railways applied paint to their cattle wagons. The small letters 'P.F.' mean 'pipe fitted' but seem to have been discontinued later. The stock of large cattle wagons to D22 was maintained at 891 from 1902 almost up to the grouping.

Ballast brake vans were painted in the normal grey livery but with vermilion red ends. In later years some at least carried the designation 'PWD' on the bottom plank of the sides, similar to the depot location. Certain sections of joint lines, such as the North Union and the Preston & Wyre Lines, were provided with a small fleet of ballast wagons and ballast brakes numbered in a separate series, but no information on lettering has come to light.

Timber trucks and bolster wagons, as well as having smaller lettering than most other goods vehicles, also had smaller diamonds, 8″ × 4″, and the bolsters themselves were numbered separately and were marked with the vehicle number and a diamond. Later the initials 'LNWR' were applied in the centre above the number, both being in 2″ characters.

The West Coast Joint Stock also owned a considerable fleet of meat and refrigerator vans which were painted similarly to their LNWR counterparts, namely grey for ordinary meat vans and white for refrigerators, the latter having grey underframes and curb rails. The WCJS solebar numberplates were oval instead of rectangular and carried the words 'WEST COAST JOINT STOCK' and the wagon number.

Because several years elapsed between successive repaintings, these various changes of detail took a considerable time to be implemented in full. Goods wagons in LNWR livery were common until about 1930 and a few examples remained in traffic until the Second World War. Wagons were also repaired and touched up at many depots around the system, as well as at the main works at Earlestown, and so detail differences in practice arose. Goods wagons were rarely photographed and thus little evidence of these variations survives, but they undoubtedly existed. Various photographs, for example, show the tare weight normally rendered as '8·9·1' but it also appears as '8-9-1' and '8.9.1'. It is thus impossible to be certain about the precise lettering details of any particular vehicle at any particular date.

LNWR wagon sheets were 19′6″ × 15′5″ in size until 1910, when they were altered to 21′6″ × 14′5″ to suit the larger high-sided wagons then in widespread use. The sheets were marked 'L&NW' and were distinguished by a red cross, but the precise arrangement is uncertain. One photograph appears to show a cross in the form of a plus sign, ' + ', about 18″ high located at the centre of each side of the sheet. A more likely arrangement is indicated in Figure 51 which has been prepared from a contemporary Bassett-Lowke model but which is not guaranteed as completely authentic, though the company usually took great trouble to get the livery details of their models correct.

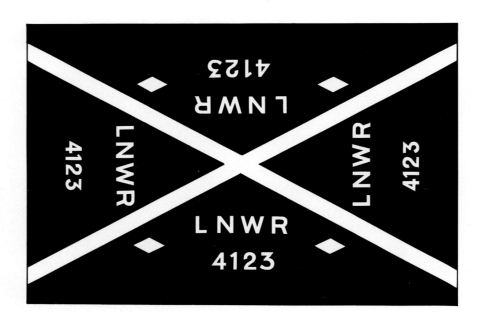

Figure 51 *(B.C. Lane)*
LNWR wagon sheet, from contemporary Bassett-Lowke model.

143

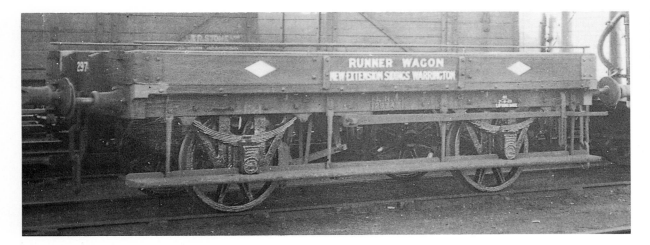

Plate 137 *(J.P.Richards. c1922)*
No. 29747 was a runner wagon converted from a low-side open to D1 and allocated to Warrington.

Plate 138 *National Railway Museum (Crown Copyright)*
10-ton goods brake van No. 234 to D16 is shown in its 1908 period livery — later the diamonds were dropped. Before this the diamonds were displayed where the 'L' and 'R' now appear. This was the standard brake van from 1870, if not earlier, until 1901 when construction ceased with 1447 in service. 288 survived to be handed over to the LMS.

Plate 139 *National Railway Museum, York*
Double-ended brake vans were rare on the LNWR. No. 982 is one of six to D18 and shows how the diamonds were located when they could not be in line with the 'LNWR' lettering, which was the preferred arrangement.

Plate 140 *(G.H.Platt collection)*
Milnes-Daimler 34-seater omnibus for working between Connah's Quay, Flint, Northop and Mold; the service commenced operation on 10th July 1905. The small lettering reads 'W. Turnbull Superintendent Euston Station Speed 12 MPH'. Passenger road vehicles replicated the LNWR carriage livery as far as possible.

145

8

ROAD VEHICLES

by **Philip Millard**

Road vehicles intended for the conveyance of passengers and parcels (as opposed to goods) were the responsibility of Wolverton works and were painted similarly to passenger carriages, except that horse buses had only three coats of varnish applied instead of the four specified for rail carriages. They were picked out in brown and lake, lining being $\frac{1}{8}''$ yellow flanked by $\frac{1}{16}''$ white. Wheel spokes were lined $\frac{1}{8}''$ down the centre in yellow, with a $\frac{1}{16}''$ white line each side of the yellow and $\frac{1}{2}''$ away from it. Horse-drawn and motor parcels vans were similar to horse buses, but had only two coats of varnish and were lined with $\frac{1}{8}''$ yellow only. Wheels of horse-drawn vans were vermilion, lined either side of the spokes, hubs and felloes in $\frac{1}{4}''$ black. On motor parcels vans the rearmost panel on each side was reserved for poster displays, and was painted ultramarine blue (normally with a poster stuck on top). On the earliest road motors the chassis appears to have been painted lake and lined out, but by 1913 the chassis was unlined varnished black. Lettering 'L&NWR EXPRESS PARCELS SERVICE' was in black, on a white ground, while the vehicle's fleet number, (for example, 12-D) was rendered in white. Some road motors carried a version of the Britannia coat of arms, which was a smaller pattern of the locomotive style of armorial transfer, $8\frac{3}{8}''$ wide and $6\frac{1}{4}''$ deep, but larger vehicles, and the horse buses, displayed the carriage transfer arms. A variety of road vehicles are illustrated in Talbot's *LNWR Miscellany* volumes.

Until early in 1911 all the goods cartage vehicles, which were constructed at Earlestown, were painted black with white lettering but thereafter a change was made to the standard chocolate brown and white, with large block 'L.& N.W.R.' lettering. At the same time the practice of fitting poster display boards came into general use. Open lorries without tilts or hoods were supplied with boards which were fixed so as to display posters above the top rail of the van sides. These boards could be removed should the load necessitate this. A poster board was fitted to the rear axle of flat drays and trollies.

An Earlestown specification dated July 1919 gives details of the painting of a pair horse delivery van to carry 4 tons:-

'All iron work to be coated over with white lead before being secured in position. The van to have three coats of best oil paint; two coats to be of lead colour, and one chocolate. Nameboards two coats white, and lettered in black L&NWR (5 inch letters).

Underwork to have three coats of red. Ironwork to be finished in drop black. To be lined and lettered as directed, and afterwards varnished with one coat of good and approved varnish.'

A similar specification refers to a lorry to carry 3 tons, and is identical except that no letter is mentioned.

On the eve of the grouping, a number of pair-horse goods vans were altered to covered meat vans, and it was specified that the lower part of the van (that is, the wooden sides)

Plate 141 *(G.H.Platt collection)*

Foden steam wagon put into service in 1905. The serif style of lettering with the name of the company spelled out in full is unusual.

Plate 142 *(G.H.Platt collection)*

Motor bus No.1, a Ford, registered in the name of the chief mechanical engineer, C.J.Bowen Cooke. It is seen here at Wolverton but is thought to have been used at Crewe Works to provide internal transport.

147

was to be painted in standard LNWR colours, the outside of the tilt and the whole of the inside, including the floor and canvas rear curtain, to be varnished white. The sides of the tilt had the words 'L.& N.W.R. MEAT VAN' in 9″ red letters, spread over two lines and 6′9″ long.

Station trucks were painted with one undercoat of red oxide, one finishing coat of quick brown, and one coat of varnish.

Plate 143 *(G.H.Platt collection)*
Motor bus No. 44, ex works at Wolverton in 1912.

148

Plate 144 *(G.H.Platt collection)*
A Ford motor van for express parcels service.

149

Plate 145 *(G.H.Platt collection)*

A Thornycroft motor van, designed to carry bicycles. The LNWR and Midland had a working agreement in many places after 1900.

150

THE OLD STYLE OF PAIR-HORSE COVERED VAN.

THE PRESENT STYLE OF PAIR-HORSE COVERED VAN, SHOWING NEW STYLE OF PAINTING, AND DISPLAYING POSTERS.

151

SINGLE-HORSE 4-WHEELED VAN FOR PASSENGER TRAIN TRAFFIC,
PAINTED, ETC., IN THE NEW STYLE.

PAIR-HORSE GOODS VAN, PAINTED IN THE NEW STYLE AND
DISPLAYING POSTERS.

THE OLD STYLE OF PAIR-HORSE VAN.

Figure 53
Another perspective drawing
dated April 1910 of the lettering applied to the numerous
fleet of light parcel carts.

153

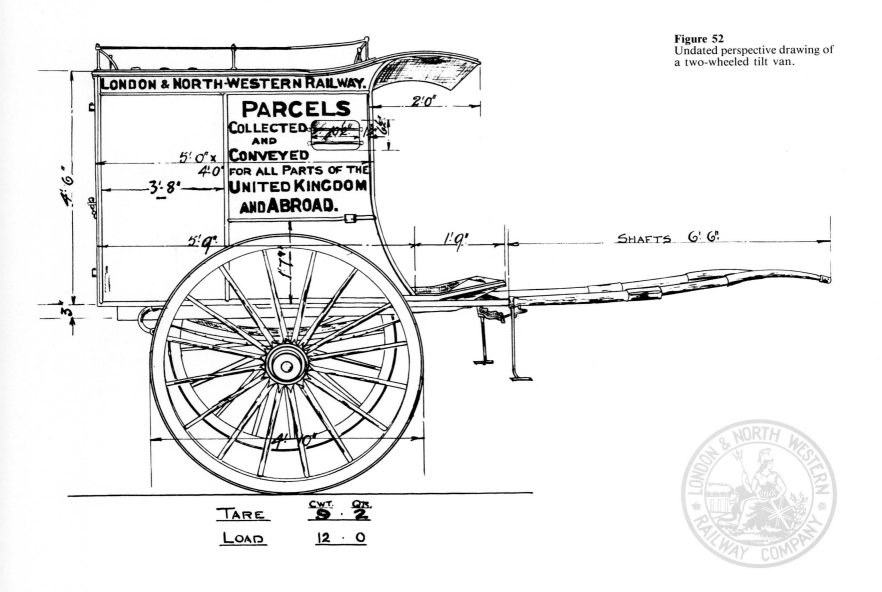

LONDON & NORTH-WESTERN RAILWAY.

PARCELS
COLLECTED
AND
CONVEYED FOR ALL PARTS OF THE
UNITED KINGDOM
AND ABROAD.

2'0"

5' 0" x
4'0"

3'.8"

5'.9"

4'.6"

3"

1'.7"

1'.9"

SHAFTS 6'.6"

4'.0"

	CWT.	QR.
TARE	9	2
LOAD	12	0

Figure 52
Undated perspective drawing of
a two-wheeled tilt van.

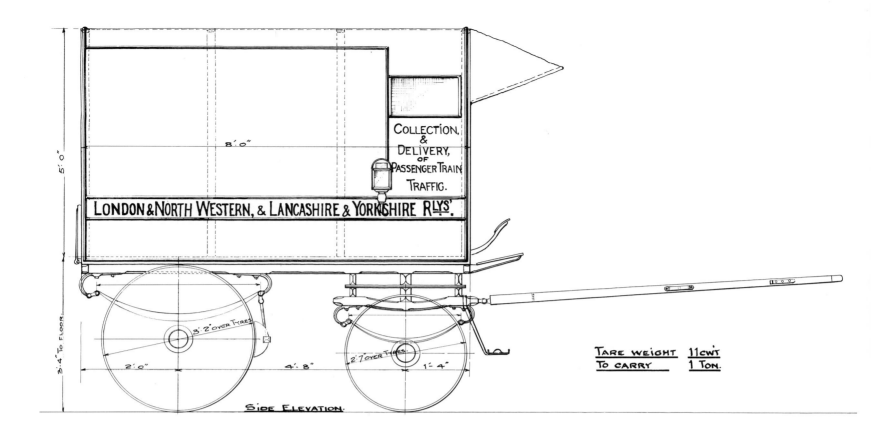

Collection,
&
Delivery,
of
Passenger Train
Traffic.

LONDON & NORTH WESTERN, & LANCASHIRE & YORKSHIRE R^{lys}.

5'0"
3'4" TO FLOOR
8'0"
3'2" OVER TYRES
2'0"
4'8"
2'7" OVER TYRES
1'4"

TARE WEIGHT   11 CWT.
TO CARRY   1 TON.

SIDE ELEVATION.

Figure 54
LNWR and LYR Joint light tilt
van for use in the Huddersfield
area. The drawing is dated October 1912.

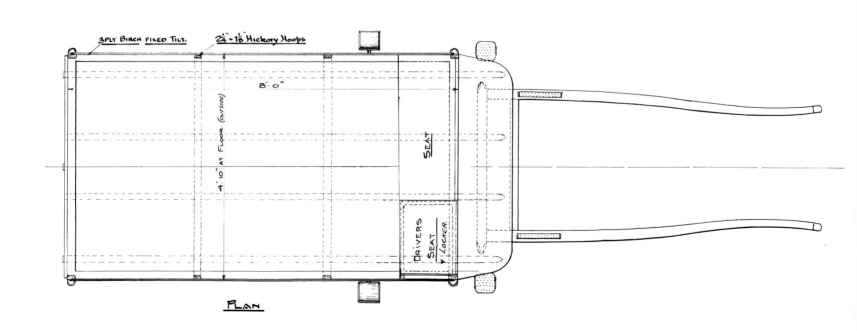

3 PLY BIRCH FIXED TILT.   2½" × 1⅛ HICKORY HOOPS

8'0"

4'10" AT FLOOR (OUTSIDE)

SEAT

DRIVERS SEAT
LOCKER

PLAN

L. N. W. R. SPECIAL LIGHT TILT VAN,   FOR   L. N. W. AND L. & Y. R^{lys} - HUDDERSFIELD.
WOLVERTON,   OCT 22ND 1912.

155

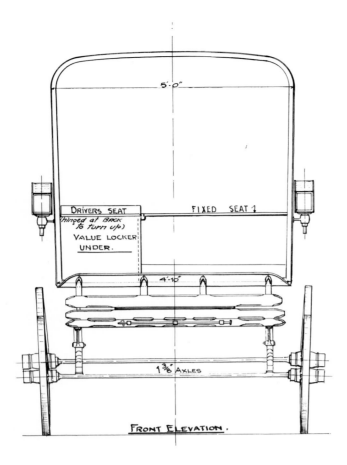

DRIVERS SEAT
(hinged at BACK
to turn up)
VALUE LOCKER
UNDER.

FIXED SEAT ?

5'·0"

4'·10"

40"

1⅜" AXLES

FRONT ELEVATION.

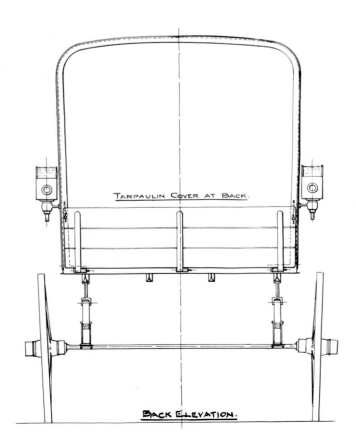

TARPAULIN COVER AT BACK.

BACK ELEVATION.

156

Plate 151
(George Dow collection)
A view of Dalston Junction about 1896. The main feature of interest is the tall signals with lattice posts and LNWR-type arms. The one on the right is lettered 'Poplar'.

9

NORTH LONDON RAILWAY

by **Philip Millard from notes by M.J.Cox**

Locomotives 1853-1885

Locomotives were painted a bright green, said to correspond with B.S.S.2660:5-064. The green was applied to the boiler, firebox, front and rear weatherboards, splasher sides, sandboxes, tank sides and ends and bunkers. The lining out consisted of a black border with a fine white line inside, while panels of varying shapes were formed by a black band with a fine white line on either side. This lining appeared on the sides and fronts of the side tanks, the sides and rear of the bunker, the outside cylinders of certain engines when painted green, and to tool-boxes when they were placed on the footplate near the smokebox. Undated photographs of Nos. 48 and 80 show what appears to be a green livery, but the corners of the panels are curved out. These seem to be isolated examples, and it is not known how long they remained thus.

The smokebox, smokebox door, chimney, footplate, splasher tops, side tank tops, well tank between the frames, brake gear, guard irons, lamp irons and all springs and hangers were painted black. Boiler bands were black, edged with white lines. When sandboxes were fitted on top of the boiler they were painted green with a black top; the top edge of the base was edged black with a white line underneath. The outside cylinders of class 1 locomotives where the wrapper is a continuation of the smokebox were black, but earlier engines had green cylinders with a panel formed by a black band edged white. Cylinder ends were at all times black.

Many parts of the engine were polished brass, and drivers and firemen took a great pride in the cleanliness and general appearance of their engines. Brass parts included the dome, the ring behind the smokebox, safety valve and base, whistle, spectacles and beading on splasher sides. On engines with raised fireboxes, the front and back cleading rings were brass and kept polished. Very early safety valves were of the brass spring balance type fitted to the polished brass dome. The large Ramsbottom safety valves fitted to engines built by Mr Adams at Bow had a polished brass base, but Mr Park introduced a smaller type of Ramsbottom valve with a painted base. Early engines also had brass beading fitted to the tank edges. All pipework in brass and copper was also polished, and the chimney caps were of polished copper. Certain steel parts, including handrails, the safety-valve lever, connecting rods and smokebox door hinges and handles, were polished bright, and it was the practice to paint the pillars at the cab entrance to a height corresponding with the rear splasher, the remainder being polished. In later years when this painted portion wore off the whole pillar was polished.

With the exception of the first batch of 0–6–0 tanks Nos. 75-80, green engines were not fitted with cabs, although Mr Park had begun to fit cabs to black painted engines in the duplicate list in 1876. On front and rear weatherboards the lining was a standard border around edge and spectacles; when cabs were fitted this style persisted, so that the

158

Plate 152
(George Dow collection)
Another view of Dalston Junction about 1896 showing NLR 4 – 4 – 0T No. 33 on a train for Broad Street. The arrangement of lining out on the rear of the bunker is clearly visible.

bunker part was panelled, leaving the top portion bordered, a feature which is not always discernible on photographs. In cases where there were no cabs, the backhead of the firebox was black and the sides red oxide.

Outside frames were claret coloured with a black border and a thin vermilion line inside. The inside surfaces of the frames were painted red oxide, and the motion plate red. Valances were vermilion edged black on the lower edge with a white line inside. Bufferbeams were also vermilion, edged black with a white line inside, and the bufferbeam ends were similarly treated. The vermilion buffer sockets had a black ring at the front end, the bufferheads being either black or polished bright.

The bosses, spokes and rims of both driving and carrying wheels were green; some photographs show wheels fully lined out for the purposes of the occasion, but no lining is discernible on the wheels of locomotives in service.

Bogie frames were green, with a black border and fine white line inside being applied continuously all round the frame, the black of the border being continued over the edge of the frame.

Coupling rods were red with the bosses polished bright, but connecting rods were unpainted and polished.

In early days the engine's number was displayed in separate polished brass figures fitted to the front of the chimney, but these, together with the polished copper chimney cap, were discontinued during Mr Park's regime.

Prior to the '43 class' of 1863, engines carried their number painted on the rear of the bunker, but thereafter a numberplate was fitted. 'Classes 21' and '30' (of 1855 and 1861) had an oval works plate on the bunker side, while 'class 38' of 1860 had a plate screwed on to the curved splasher. Engines of 'class 43' and 'class 51' had the building information incorporated in the splasher plate. In 1873 the standard rectangular number plate made of brass with raised numerals, letters and edge on a black ground was introduced; the plates fitted to the side tanks had, in addition to the number, the initials 'N.L.R.', the word 'BUILT' or 'REBUILT' and the date and works. The plate fitted to the rear of the bunker was exactly the same, except that only the engine number was displayed; the model of No. 60 in the National Railway Museum is incorrect in this respect, having a side type plate fitted at the rear. The numberplate fitted to No. 75, the first of the 0–6–0T engines built for goods working in 1879, gave the building date as 1881 but the reason for this mistake is not known. This engine was at first fitted with a stovepipe chimney, which after a short period was replaced by one of standard pattern.

From 1875, soon after Mr Park took over as Locomotive Superintendent, locomotives of the inside cylinder '43 class' on the duplicate list were painted black; lining consisted of a single panel on tanks and bunker formed by a thin red line, although another source quotes double red lines.

A minute of the locomotive, stores and traffic committee dated 26th June 1885 recommended the adoption of black as the standard colour for engines, 'as experience of the last nine years with the inside cylinder engines shows that colour to be not only more durable and less costly than green, but easier to keep clean'. The proposal was approved, but engines were still to be seen in the green livery after 1885; the late Mr J.F.Vickery recorded that Nos. 11 and 12 were painted that colour in 1886, while a few were still to be seen as late as 1890.

Locomotives 1885-1922

From 1885 until the line was absorbed by the LNWR on 1st January 1922, the locomotives were painted black overall. The lining was more ornate than had been used with the green livery and consisted of a blue-grey border with a chrome yellow line on the inside, and a panel formed of a blue-grey band with a chrome yellow line on either side. A thin red line was placed a short distance inside the yellow one. This lining was

160

applied to the sides and fronts of the side tanks, the sides and rear of the bunker and to the sandboxes. Lining was also applied to the cab front, sides and rear, and round the polished brass spectacles, but there was no lining on the footsteps. Boiler bands were black with two red lines, while valances and frames were edged blue-grey with a red line inside.

With effect from 1st February 1908, the line, although remaining independent, was managed by LNWR officers reporting to the NLR board of directors. From this time onwards engines began to appear with lining very similar to the LNWR style; the border disappeared leaving the main panel with its blue-grey band and inside red line. Lining ceased to be applied to the front of the side tanks and to the sandboxes which were now plain black, but a panel of blue-grey and yellow line appeared on the cab side sheet in typically LNWR fashion.

During this period, the following parts were polished brass: ring behind smokebox, whistle, spectacles and pipework. Handrails and pillars were polished bright steel, as were the safety valve easing lever, the buffer heads, the connecting rods and the bosses of the coupling rods. The coupling rods themselves remained red, as in the earlier period.

161

The inside of the frames and the motion plate were painted red, but outside cylinders were plain black, unlined. The bogie frames of inside-cylinder passenger engines were edged blue-grey with a red line on the inside, but the bogie frames of engines which had outside cylinders were unlined. Bufferbeams were vermilion, edged black, and buffer sockets were also black. The ends of the bufferbeams were black, bordered in blue-grey with a fine red line inside, but in some cases the bufferbeam end was plain. The number of the engine was painted on the bufferbeam in gold characters shaded black thus 'N⁰ 70', but after 1909 this was discontinued and the bufferbeam was plain vermilion.

Numberplates remained of the 1873 rectangular pattern, and as before the plate on the rear of the bunker specified the engine number only. The plates displayed polished brass lettering and border on a black ground, but after 1909 the ground was changed to red and the letters LNWR took the place of NLR. A blue-grey line surrounded the numberplate until 1909. From 1895 onwards the company's coat of arms was displayed beneath the numberplate on the side tanks of the passenger engines only. On the model of No. 60 the coat of arms is incorrectly located on the bunker. Although there exists a photograph of an 0−6−0T, No. 17, showing the coat of arms, it is believed that this was applied for photographic purposes only. No works plates were carried. Cab interiors were red oxide until about 1909, but from that date the top half was red-brown and the bottom half was painted black.

The destination boards carried over the bufferbeams were black, with white letters. Daytime head codes took the form of various iron plates or discs displayed on the left-hand side of the chimney (a position changed to the top of the smokebox in later years) and over the buffers. When running bunker first the plates were carried centrally at the top of the bunker and over the buffers. At night lamps were carried in corresponding positions.

Carriages

During the whole of the NLR's existence, the sides and ends of carriages were varnished teak, lined in gold. The ends of passenger luggage vans and brake ends were painted vermilion, while roofs were white, rapidly becoming dark grey. Underframes were also of varnished wood, with the ironwork painted bronze brown. The wood centres of Mansell wheels were also varnished, steel parts being black. Carriages built by the LNWR at Wolverton in 1910-12 were finished in a similar manner (although in dark Burma teak rather than the lighter coloured wood previously employed), but in this case the underframes were made of steel and painted black. Furthermore, the brake ends were not painted vermilion on these carriages. In all cases, metal underframe parts such as brake gear and gas cylinders were painted black.

In most cases the carriage number was painted on the panel above the quarterlights, but on the Wolverton-built carriages the number was transferred to the waist and rendered in serif numerals. Bow-built carriages employed block style numerals; sometimes the carriage number was displayed by itself, sometimes the prefix N⁰ was used, and in yet other cases the letters 'N.L.R.' appeared.

The gilt letters and numerals were edged round with fine lines; black, white and blue for the first class and black, white and red for the inferior classes. One source claims that red shading was used for letters and numerals but none is visible in photographs.

The compartment class designation was indicated in gold block letters on the door at waist height; carriages built at Bow had an elliptical raised panel on the doors, and this was decorated with the company's coat of arms in the case of first-class compartments. The panels on the doors of inferior classes, and also guards' brake vans, were decorated with the company's intertwined initials in the form of a monogram, but on some third-class carriages this was replaced by a large serif figure '3' with a flat top, which appeared in addition to the word 'THIRD'. The words 'GUARD'S COMPT' (later altered to the single word 'GUARD') appeared as appropriate. The Wolverton-built carriages had their class designations on the doors in large numerals of the same pattern as used by the LNWR for its own 'brown trains' used on the Mansion House services. Here the 3's had rounded tops. Two coats of arms were also applied to the lower panels.

Carriages built before 1910 had an oval works plate fitted to the solebar, but the Wolverton carriages followed LNWR detailed practice. Side lamps were painted red, and destination boards were white with a black edge and black lettering.

Plate 155   *(G.H.Platt collection)*
NLR third No. 87, also one of the Wolverton-built vehicles, photographed soon after the grouping. The centre compartment has a 'non-smoking' label.

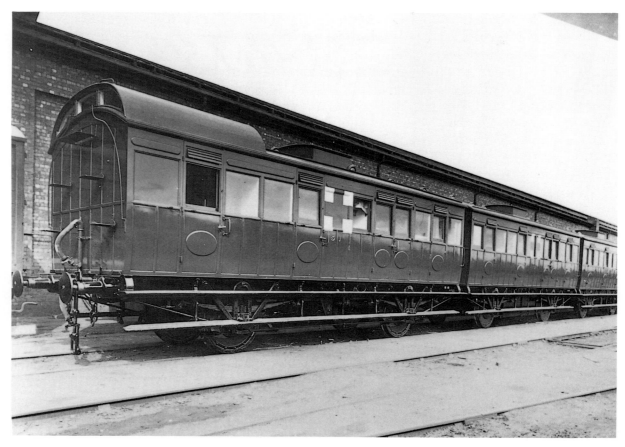

Plate 156   *(G.H.Platt collection)*
In May 1917 the NLR sold a train of older carriages to the government for use as an ambulance train at Salonica. This train, Overseas Ambulance Train No. 38, did not return after the war. The leading vehicle is brake infections car No. S1 which had been altered from NLR first class No. 91, originally built in 1905. The train was painted in khaki with red-on-white Geneva crosses.

163

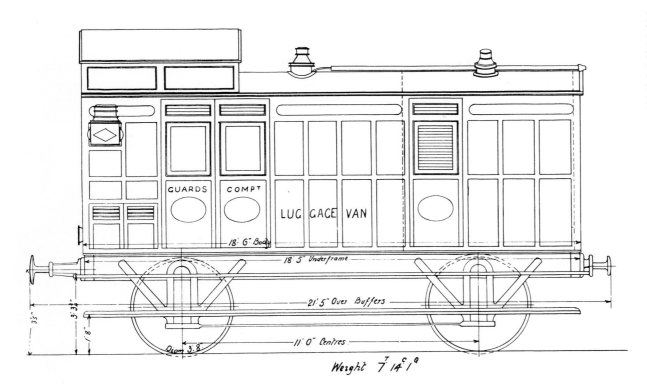

GUARDS COMPT

LUGGAGE VAN

18' 6" Body

18' 5" Underframe

21' 5" Over Buffers

3' 3¾"

3' 5"

1' 8"

Diam 3' 8"

11' 0" Centres

Weight 7 14 1

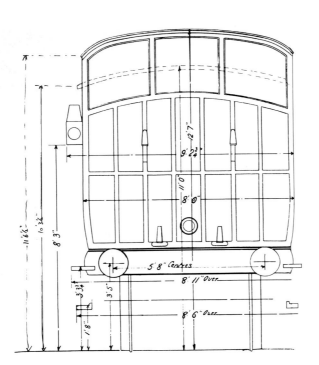

2' 7"

9' 6¾"

11' 0"

8' 0"

11' 6½"

10' 3½"

8' 3"

3' 3¾"

3' 5"

1' 8"

5' 8" Centres

8' 11" Over

8' 6" Over

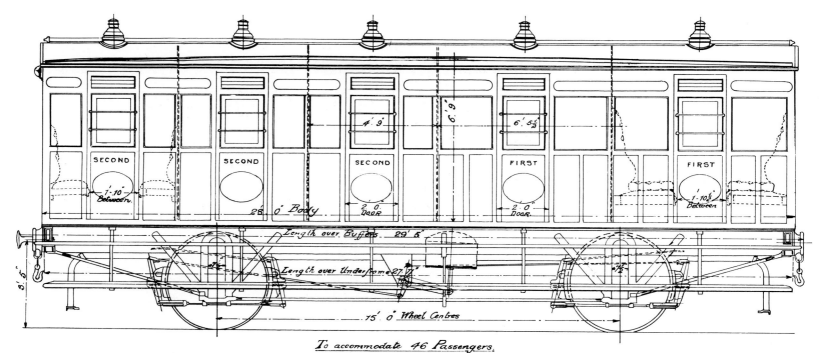

SECOND SECOND SECOND FIRST FIRST

1'·10"
Between

28'·0" Body

4'·9"

6'·9"

6'·5½"

2'·0"
Door

2'·0"
Door

1'·10½"
Between

Length over Buffers 29'·5"

5'·5"

Length over Underframe 27'·7"

15'·0" Wheel Centres

To accommodate 46 Passengers.

Weight empty 9 . 15 . 3
                T   C   Q

Diagram of N.L. Composite Carriage. 28'·0" × 8'·0". (Low Roof.)

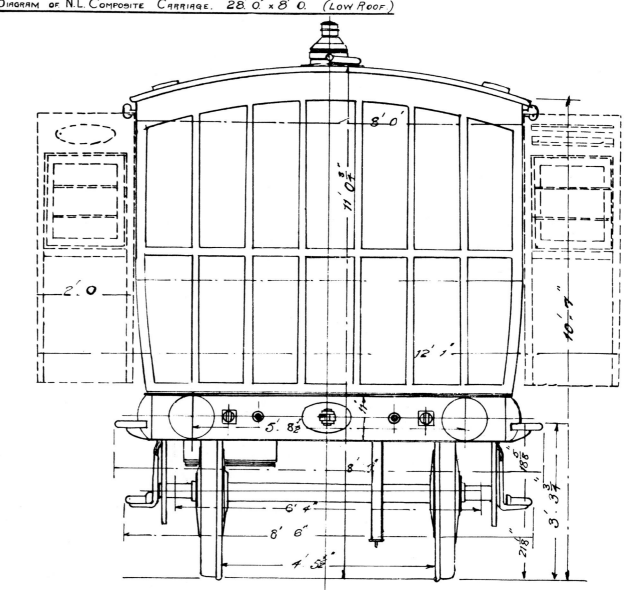

8'·0"

11'·0⅜"

10'·7"

2'·0"

12'·1"

5'·8½"

8'·1"

188"

3'·3⅞"

6'·4"

21⅜"

8'·6"

4'·5½"

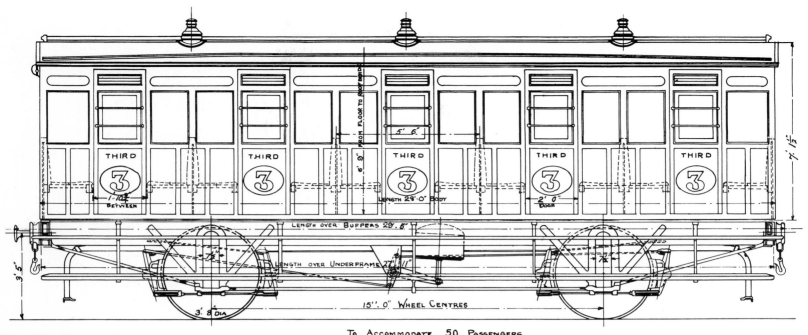

To Accommodate 50 Passengers.
Weight Empty 8.18.0

— L. N. W. Rʸ. Cᵒ. —

DIAGRAM OF N.L. 28'. 0" THIRD CLASS CARRIAGE (LOW ROOF)

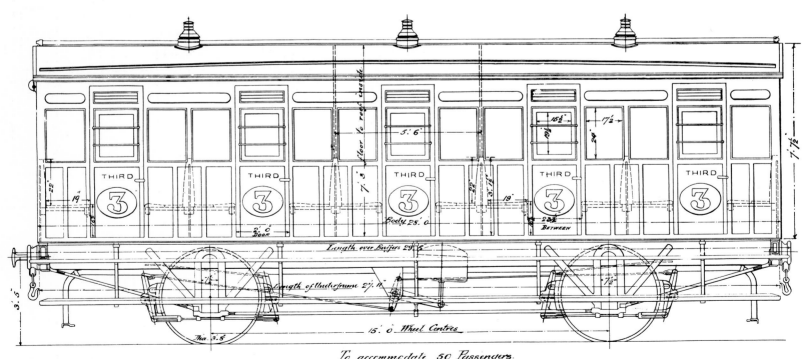

To accommodate 50 Passengers.
Weight Empty 9. 4. 3

Diagram of Third Class Carriage. (High Roof.)

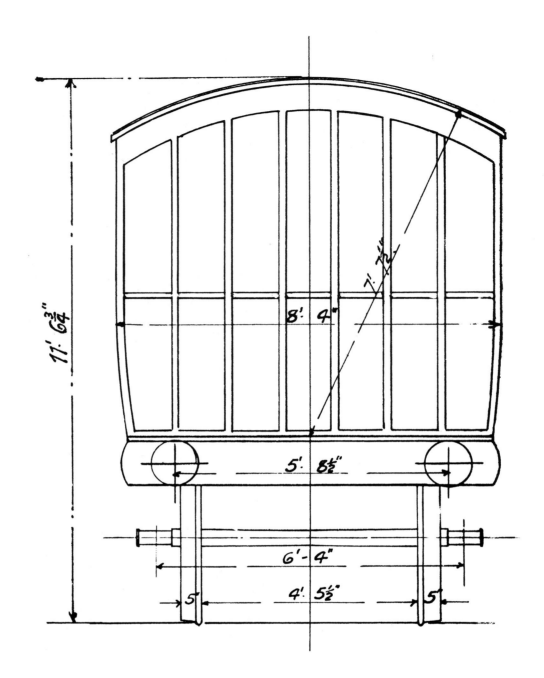

11' 6¾"

8' 4"

7' 7½"

5' 8½"

6' - 4"

4' 5½"

5'   5'

167

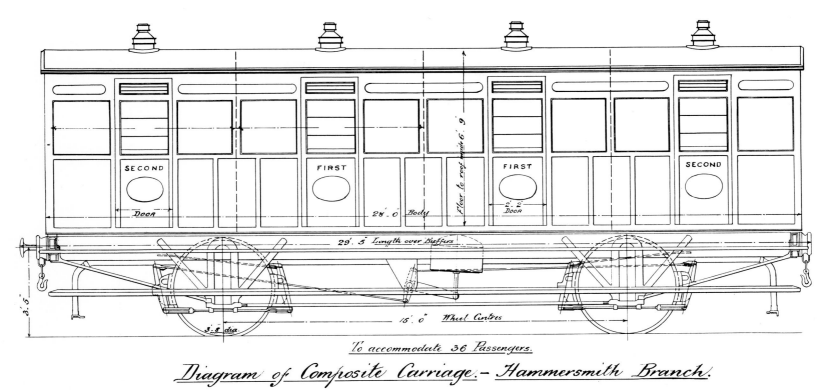

To accommodate 36 Passengers.

Diagram of Composite Carriage.- Hammersmith Branch.

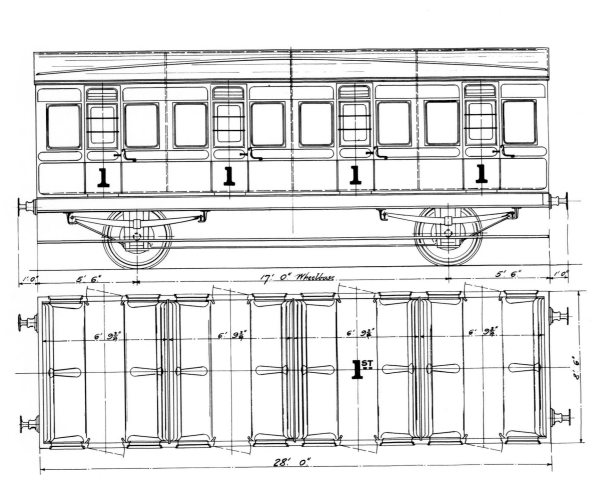

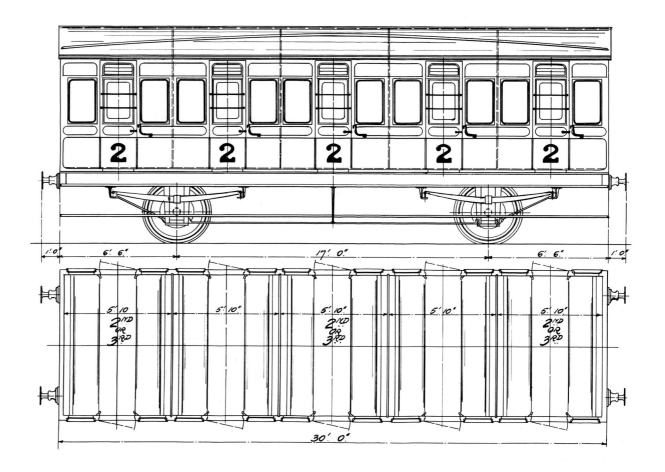

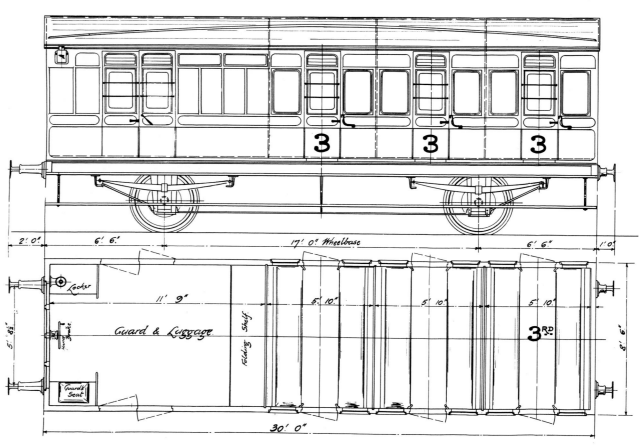

169

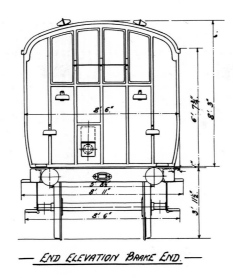

— *END ELEVATION BRAKE END.* —

Goods Wagons

Goods wagons were painted a very dark grey, almost black, with white lettering. The company's initials were always rendered 'N.L.R' one plank deep, with the wagon number in characters of the same size. All wagons carried a cast-iron number-plate painted black, with 'N.L.R', the number and date and place of building picked out in white. The raised border of the plate was also white.

Other details

Few other details of NLR painting practices are extant; signals followed standard LNWR practice after 1909, while stations were painted light yellow.

No 790 HARDWICKE (lower) and 'Coal Tank' No. 1054 (upper) photographed at the Dinting Railway Centre, Derbyshire, on 3 October 1982 by Edward Talbot.

EPILOGUE

by **Edward Talbot**

The LNWR Today

The following list contains details of items of LNWR origin which were known to exist in mid 1985.

Engines

'6ft Single' No. 1868, formerly COLUMBINE, at the National Railway Museum, York. Restored to black livery with 1873-6 lining and no cab. It is unlikely that it ever ran in this condition, as it was renumbered 1868 in December 1871, before the black livery was introduced, was rebuilt in 1875, when the cab is thought to have been added, and became ENGINEER BANGOR in November 1877. Nevertheless, its present condition is the best compromise available, and it is a fascinating exhibit. The inside of the frames is black.

'8ft 6in Single' No. 3020 CORNWALL, National Railway Museum, York. Recently re-painted for a tour to Japan, with dome polished brass as in 1920. The inside of the frames is red.

'4ft Shunter' No. 1439, National Railway Museum, York. Its condition is as withdrawn from industrial service in 1954, with many Webb fittings and in a dubious attempt at the pre-1873 green livery, with white lining as well as black, red bufferbeams and so forth.

'6ft 6in Jumbo' No. 790 HARDWICKE, National Railway Museum, York. Its condition is basically as withdrawn by the LMS but restored to LNWR livery after World War II. Errors are the red bufferbeam on the tender, instead of black, and the post-1915 '9' on the numberplate. The inside of the frames is red.

'Coal Tank' No. 1054, Dinting Railway Centre, Derbyshire. The engine is beautifully restored to Webb condition. The inside of the frames is red.

'G2' 0–8–0 LMS No. 9395 (LNWR No. 485), owned by the National Railway Museum, York, but out-stationed at Ironbridge Gorge Museum, Blists Hill, Telford. Its condition is basically as withdrawn by BR in November 1959 but it has been allowed to deteriorate badly due to long exposure to the elements, only half-hearted attempts at restoration and official neglect in general.

PET, 18in-gauge Crewe Works shunter, in the Narrow Gauge Railway Museum, Talyllyn Railway, Towyn.

Constituent and Associated Companies

ROCKET, Liverpool & Manchester Railway 0−2−2, Science Museum, London.

SANSPAREIL, Liverpool & Manchester Railway 0−4−0, Science Museum, London.

SHANNON, 0−4−0WT built by George England in 1857 for the Sandy & Potton Railway, which was absorbed by the LNWR in 1862. Sold to the Wantage Tramway in 1878 and now preserved at Didcot.

North London Railway 0−6−0 tank No. 76, LNWR 2650, now restored in BR black livery as No. 58850 on the Bluebell Railway.

Carriages

13′ 5½″ horse box, built c1865, at Leighton Buzzard.

Queen Victoria's 60′ saloon, LMS 802, National Railway Museum, York.

21′ passenger full brake, body only, on private land at Bletchley.

Four-wheeled observation saloon No. 68, built in 1877 for the Blaenau Festiniog-Llandudno Junction branch until replaced by the vehicle now on the Bluebell Railway. Only the body remains, devoid of all fittings except the original internal sliding doors. Bow ended. In poor condition but restorable. At Quainton Road.

Two 5-compartment thirds, bodies only, now used as shops at Quainton Road. The length and diagram are not known but the bolection mouldings are pre-1887. Very little of the originals is left, only the end and side walls of the bodies, and the double-skinned floors. Gas lit.

30′1″ brake third body to D361, built about 1890, in BR service at Wolverton.

21′ underframe at Wolverton.

57′ eight-wheeled Semi Royal clerestory saloon to D1 No. 806. Privately preserved, location not known.

65′6″ dining saloon built in 1900 to D29, LMS 76, National Railway Museum, York.

65′6″ dining saloon built in 1901 to D29, LMS No. 77, but now restored to pristine LNWR condition at Quainton Road. Used by servants in Royal Train 1916-1966.

65′6″ King Edward's saloon, LMS No. 800, National Railway Museum, York.

65′6″ Queen Alexandra's saloon, LMS No. 801, National Railway Museum, York.

57′ corridor first brake built in 1905 to D127A, LMS No. 5154, formerly in the Royal Train, National Railway Museum, York.

57′ corridor brake first built in 1905 to D127A, LMS No. 5155, formerly in the Royal Train, National Railway Museum, York.

65′6″ sleeping saloon built about 1908 to D16, LNWR No. 112. Converted to Instruc-

173

tional Staff Cinema coach by 1923 and withdrawn in 1973. Undergoing external repanelling as cinema car at Quainton Road.

50′ TPO built in 1909 to D391, LNWR No. 20, later 9520, LMS No. 3227, later 30244. Originally gas lit. Condition poor. Owned by the National Railway Museum, York, but located at Tyseley (previously at Chasewater).

57′ third brake non-corridor toplight built in 1917 to D333, BR No. M22687M, Railway Preservation Society, Chasewater.

57′ third brake toplight built in 1921 to D333 or D333A, LNWR No. 7340, LMS No. 7107, BR No. 22736, at Quainton Road. Converted to riding and mess van in May 1958, allocated to Bletchley breakdown crew as DM 395209. Now used as mess coach; still has full LNWR axleboxes.

30′1″ six-wheeled passenger full brake built about 1890 to D385, the only survivor of 290. Still retains full LNWR undergear, leather diaphragm vacuum cylinder, gas tanks, and so forth. Withdrawn in 1952 as DM 279982, C&W batteries store van at Wolverton. In regular use on vintage train at Quainton Road; awaits final lining out but needs rebuilding.

30′ six-wheeled combination truck to D444, National Railway Museum, York.

32′ inspection saloon, LMS No. 45021, was on the Severn Valley Railway, now bought by the Kent & East Sussex Railway.

50′ passenger full brake built in 1905 to D377 (or perhaps WCJS DW79), Railway Preservation Society, Chasewater.

66′6″ Directors' Saloon LMS No. 45002, built in 1914 to D2. Resembles 1908 2pm 'Corridor' stock. Midland & Great Northern Railway, Sheringham.

57′ observation saloon built in 1912/13 to M50, LMS No. 15843. Now restored to pristine condition on the Bluebell Railway.

57′ composite built in 1920 to D131, LNWR No. 2997. Converted to riding and tool van in 1955 as DM 395136. Awaits restoration at Quainton Road.

50′ Ward Car built in 1916 to D378C for Home Ambulance Train No. 7. Converted to full brake in 1921. LNWR No. 8898, LMS 2362, later 32745, BR CND 395455. Still in BR service as a tool van and located on up side north of Watford Junction.

Fruit and Milk van, National Railway Museum, York.

Combination truck — 'Elephant Van' — after use by Barnum & Bailey's circus, BR No. CND 395080, now serves as site volunteer accommodation, Quainton Road.

Similar vehicle to above on Lakeside & Haverthwaite Railway in similar use due to its design.

Covered carriage truck built in 1916 to D444A, LNWR No. 12196, LMS No. 36966, later 4183, London Midland & Scottish Steam Preservation Group, Swanage.

Covered carriage truck bult in 1922 to D444A, LNWR No. 12220, Severn Valley Railway, Bewdley.

174

Pooley Van built in 1921, BR No. 395273, on Severn Valley Railway.

42′ dining saloon, built in 1891 and became LMS No. 5159. Recently rescued from a house in Bognor, restored and now in use with the Great Scottish & Western Railway on charter in Scotland.

'Oerlikon' electric open third brake motor coach built in 1915, LMS No. 28249, National Railway Museum, York.

WCJS

32′ six-wheeled sleeping/day saloon No. 102, built in 1874 in a batch of six. Converted to inspection saloon and allocated to Engineer Bangor in 1903; became LMS No. 010393, later 45624, and withdrawn in 1945. Body only awaits restoration at Quainton Road but is substantially complete, with all external and many internal fittings. The oldest WCJS item and the oldest public use sleeping car.

42′ radial TPO to DW87, No. 186, National Railway Museum, York.

65′6″ dining saloon No. 484 built in 1897 but later rebuilt with an observation end as an engineer's saloon, becoming LMS 45018. Owned by W.H.McAlpine and located at Steamtown, Carnforth.

Constituent and Associated Companies

Six Liverpool & Manchester Railway carriages, replicas built in 1930 of 1834 vehicles, National Railway Museum, York.

Grand Junction Railway, replica of 1838 TPO on wagon frame, National Railway Museum, York.

London & Birmingham Railway, Queen Adelaide's saloon, No. 2, built in 1842, National Railway Museum, York.

Dundalk, Newry & Greenore Railway composite coupé No. 1. Built at Wolverton in 1901 to LNWR pattern, 34′6″ long, 5′3″ gauge. Has $2\frac{1}{2}$ first-class compartments and two second-class, with coupé end windows. Carried LNWR style livery until withdrawal in the 1960s. Owned by and located at the Belfast Folk & Transport Museum.

Duke of Sutherland's saloon built in 1899, No. 57A, National Railway Museum, York.

North London Railway four-wheeled brake third built at Wolverton in 1910. Kent & East Sussex Railway.

Wagons

10 ton 18′ covered van to D88 at SRPS, Falkirk.

10 ton 18′ covered van to D88 body only on private land near Banbury.

Four-plank open wagon lettered 'LNWR' but not a genuine LNWR vehicle, Ironbridge Gorge Museum, Blists Hill, Telford.

15 ton boiler trolley 'Flatrol' built 1911, on Kent & East Sussex Railway.

175

RECTANK to D109 at Toddington.

WARFLAT to D110 (perhaps not LNWR but identical) in service with BR Engineering.

20 ton goods brake van to D17, Tyseley.

20 ton goods brake van to D17A, Conway Valley Museum, Bettws-Y-Coed.

20 ton goods brake van to D17B, Prestatyn.

20 ton goods brake van to D17B, Cranmore.

20 ton goods brake van on Kent & East Sussex Railway.

Narrow-gauge wagons ex Crewe Works, at Conway Valley Museum, Bettws-Y-Coed.

Narrow-gauge slate wagon, built in 1887, LMS No. 284465, in Narrow Gauge Railway Museum, Towyn.

Narrow-gauge wagons, at least two types, at Festiniog mine.

Other

Goods brake van, perhaps NLR, at Ironbridge.

Departmental Stock

Steam breakdown crane No. 2987, built in 1908, owned by the National Railway Museum and located at Carnforth.

Match truck No. 284235, built in 1907, owned by the National Railway Museum and located at Carnforth.

Signalling

Some 150 LNWR signal cabins with LNWR lever frames are still in use on BR, some dating back to the 1880s. A few LNWR block instruments and ground signals are also still in BR service.

Preservation

Type 5 signal cabin and tappet lever frame, built in 1907, at Nene Valley Railway, Wansford.

Type 4 signal cabin and tumbler lever frame, built 1898, at Shackerstone Light Railway, Market Bosworth.

Type 4 wooden signal cabin from Yorton, at Severn Valley Railway, Arley.

National Railway Museum, York has the following lever frames:
Overhead S4 type tumbler from Mossley.
Overhead S4 type tumbler from Chester No. 6.
Overhead type Crewe System power frame built in 1906 from Crewe Station A.
Standard type Crewe System power frame from Gresty Lane No. 1 (the first one built, in 1899).

Miscellaneous

Wolverton tender frame and cylindrical tank in BR service at Machynlleth.

Wolverton & Stony Stratford Tramway, various items at Stacy Hill Museum.

Hand crane, possibly two, at Butterley.

Water tank at Highley from Hadley on the Stafford-Wellington line.

Water tower at Haverthwaite.

London & Birmingham Railway stone sleepers used for the platform edging at Bicester (London Road) station (LNWR).

Grand Junction Railway stone sleepers on abutment of first overbridge north of Stafford station.

BIBLIOGRAPHY

Many books on the LNWR have been published over the years. The following is a selection of those containing information on liveries.

Baughan, Peter E. **The Chester & Holyhead Railway Vol 1** *David & Charles, Newton Abbot, 1972.*

Casserley, R.M. and Millard, P.A. **A Register of West Coast Joint Stock** *Historical Model Railway Society, 1980.*

Foster, Richard D. **A Pictorial Record of LNWR Signalling** *Oxford Publishing Company, Poole, 1982.*

Hambleton, F.C. **Locomotives Worth Modelling** *Model & Allied Publications, Hemel Hempstead, 1977.*

Hawkins, Chris and Reeve, George, **LMS Engine Sheds Vol 1: The LNWR** *Wild Swan Publications, Upper Bucklebury, Berkshire, 1981.*

Jenkinson, David **An Illustrated History of LNWR Coaches** *Oxford Publishing Company, Oxford, 1978.*

Maskelyne, J.N. **Locomotives I Have Known** *Model & Allied Publications, Hemel Hempstead, 1980.*

Nelson, Jack **LNWR Portrayed** *Peco Publications, Seaton, Devon, 1975.*

Reed, Brian **Crewe Locomotive Works and Its Men** *David & Charles, Newton Abbot, 1982.*

Reed Brian **Loco Profile No. 15 The Crewe Type** *Profile Publications, Windsor, 1971.*

Talbot, Edward **An Illustrated History of LNWR Engines** *Oxford Publishing Company, Poole, 1985.*

Talbot, Edward **LNWR Miscellany Vol 1** *Oxford Publishing Company, Oxford, 1978.*

Talbot, Edward **LNWR Miscellany Vol 2** *Oxford Publishing Company, Oxford, 1980.*

Webster, Norman W. **Britain's First Trunk Line** *Adams & Dart, Bath, 1972.*

West,W. **The Train Makers** *Barracuda Books, Buckingham 1982.*

The North London Railway: A Pictorial Record *HMSO, 1979.*

INDEX

A

Armorial devices
  DNGR   1, 2, 5
  LNWR   carriages   1, 3
            locomotives   1, 3, 70
            road vehicles   1, 2, 4, 6
            steamships   1, 4
  NLR   2, 6
  WCJS   88

B

Ballast wagons   139, 141
Banana vans   139
Bassett-Lowke   129, 143
Bessemer steel   8
Betley Road   9
Boundary posts   13, 16
Brightwork
  Bury engines   43, 49
  connecting rods   54, 72
  copper chimney caps   44, 49
  coupling rods   53, 72
  McConnell engines   49
  'Parts finished bright'   53, 72
Britannia   1, 2, 94
Bufferbeams
  front   54, 70, 71
  rear   60, 70
Buildings   26
Buttons, staff uniform
  LNWR   2
  NLR   2

C

Cab interiors
  buff   71
  crew's names displayed   71
  grained oak   71
  indian red   71
Carmarthen branch   26

Carriages
  'American Special'   102
  bolection mouldings   91
  Bolton & Leigh   86
  clerestory sides   95
  cove-roof stock, 1903   92
  dining saloons   92, 102, 123
  end steps   92
  gangways   91, 116
  GNR, teak   88
  GJR   86
  handles   92
  L&BR   86-7
  L&MR   86
  Lancaster & Preston Junction   87
  Manchester & Birmingham   87
  'Mansion House' stock   103, 115, 163
  mouldings   90, 92
  NLR   162-70
  North Union   86
  Northern Division   87
  Oerlikon electric stock   123
  roofs   95
  royal saloons   93, 103
  sleeping saloons   92, 102, 123
  Southern Division   87
  spring blinds   117
  workmen's   103
  '2pm Corridor' stock   92, 102
Carriage sheds   38
Carriage trucks   105, 123
Chalk Farm   8
Class designations   123, 162
Cleaning instructions   72
Coal bonus scheme   71
Colours, see Paints
Connecting rods   54, 72
Continuous brakes   117, 139
Continuous welded rail   9
Coupling rods   53, 72, 160
Covered trucks   105, 123
Creosote   8, 10, 13, 128

D

Destination boards   115, 162
Diamond symbols   129, 131, 135, 141, 143

Divisions
  North Eastern   42
  Northern   42-3
  Southern   42-5

E

Earl of Lichfield   20

Elmhurst Crossing   7

Engine builders
  Bury, Curtis & Kennedy   43-4
  Jones & Potts   44
  Kitson   45
  Sharp Brothers   44
  Sharp Stewart   48
  Tayleur   48
  Vulcan Foundry   49

Engineering Districts   139-40

Exhibitions
  International 1862   8
  Manchester Jubilee 1887   57

F

Fencing
  lineside   13
  platform   13, 27, 31
  roadside   13

Fire buckets   27

Floor coverings
  carpets   117, 122, 123
  Decolite   123
  Kork   123

Footbridges   29, 30

Foulger, Messrs   47

Frames   71

G

Gates
  level crossing   40
  occupation   35

Goods sheds   26

Gradient indicators   13, 15, 17

H

Hademore Crossing   19

Hibernia   1

Horseboxes   105

I

ICI   50

L

Lamps
  electric   33
  gas   32, 37
  oil   31, 36
  station   31
  yard   38

Leather
  in carriages   117, 121
  Moroccan   117

Lettering
  carriages   92-4
  carriages, NLR   162-3
  DACHSHUND   73
  solebars   115
  tank engines   72-3
  wagons   131, 136
  waist panels   94-5

Level crossings   40

Loading gauges   40

Lining
  boiler bands   50, 52, 61, 63-4
  cessation in 1914   57
  double black   52
  footplating   61, 63-4
  goods engines   57
  NLR   158, 160-1
  panels   61-8
  resumption in 1921   58
  'Special DX'   57
  splashers   63-70
  tenders   52, 60, 62
  '18″ Goods'   57

Locomotive Liveries
  CORONATION   78, 81, 84
  GJR   43, 49
  GLADSTONE   83
  GREATER BRITAIN, scarlet   81-2
  green to black 1871-3   43, 54-6

L&BR 43
North Eastern Division 42
Northern Division 43, 47, 50, 52
PATRIOT 84
QUEEN EMPRESS, white 81-3
SHAH OF PERSIA 55
Southern Division, green 43-6
Southern Division, red 43, 46-7
wartime 57-8

Locomotives
'Benbow' 70
'Bill Bailey' 68, 70
'Bloomers' 45-6, 48, 58
'Claughton' 57-8, 61, 70-2
COLUMBINE 61, 70
CORNWALL 57
COURIER 49
compound tanks 57
Cramptons 44
'DX' 50, 52-3, 56, 70
'George the Fifth' 57, 70
'Greater Britain' 81
JOHN RAMSBOTTOM 54
LADY OF THE LAKE 49, 53
LIVERPOOL 44
NEWTON 50
'Old Crewe' types 50, 53, 57
PIONEER 55-6
'Prince of Wales' 57, 67, 70
'Precursor' 72
'Precursor Tank' 57, 70, 72-3
'Problem' 50-1, 67
SAMSON 50
SHAH OF PERSIA 56, 70, 81
Sharp singles 47
'Special DX' 67
'Special Tank' 53-4, 57
Square saddle tank 57, 62-3
S.R. GRAVES 55
'Superheater tank' 57, 72

WAVERLEY 55
0-4-0ST 50, 52-3
0-4-2T 57
'18" Goods' 57, 67
'19" Goods' 67, 70
'7'6" Patent' 45-6, 48

Locomotive sheds, see Steam Sheds

M

McConnell tenders 45-6

Mansell wheels 95, 162

Maple & Co 122

Mileage indicators 13, 15-17

Minutes
loco committee 58, 94
stores committee 129
traffic committee 141
Monograms, carriages
LNWR 94
WCJS 94, 105

N

Nameplates
cast 78-80
CORONATION 78, 81, 84
early types 49
LIVERPOOL 49
LONDON 49
PATRIOT 78, 80, 84
returned to Crewe 49
standard curved 76-7
standard straight 77-8
Webb compounds 76, 78
18" gauge shunters 76

Naming
carriages 86
cessation in 1917 57-8
goods engines 53
resumption in 1921 58

Naphtholine 128

North London Railway
carriages 162
locomotives 158, 160-2
signals 20, 170
stations 170
wagons 170

Notices 32-4, 39

Numberplates
bridges 13, 18
engines 48, 53, 73
NLR 162
property 18
Southern Division 48
standard numerals 74
tenders 75, 79
wagons 137, 143
Webb cast-iron 73-4
Webb brass 73-4
Whale 73-4
1915 '6' and '9' 73, 79

Numbers
on carriages
LNWR 89, 93, 97, 123
royal saloons 93
WCJS 89, 93, 102, 123

on engines
  L&BR 47
  L&MR 47
  on bufferbeams 47-8
  on chimneys 47-8
  painted 47

O

Occupation crossings 35

P

Paints and Colours
  'blackberry black' 61
  brown 19, 24
  brunswick green 45
  buff 19, 24
  burnt sienna 126
  carbolineum 24
  carmine lake 126
  chocolate 90
  claret 88-90
  dark grey 128
  drab 88
  drop black 61, 125-6
  flake white 61, 90, 125
  gold leaf 72, 90
  gold powder 93, 126
  indian red 71, 105, 125
  invisible green 55
  lake 88-92, 105
  lemon chrome 90
  lining colours: red, cream and grey 61
  maroon 89
  medium green 43, 50
  mid grey 128
  orange chrome 90
  oxide of iron 47
  quaker green 88
  quick brown 105, 148
  primer 26
  turkey umber 24, 105, 126
  ultramarine blue 61, 90, 125-6
  venetian red 91-2
  vermilion 24, 61, 71-2, 126
  white lead 24, 90, 125
  yellow 90
  yellow chrome 160
  yellow ochre 24, 61, 72-3, 90, 126
  zinc white 126

Paint specifications, carriages 125-6

Panelling, Wolverton traditional 91

Parliamentary trains 88

Permanent way
  constituent and subsidiary companies
    Chester & Holyhead 8
    Crewe & Chester 8
    Grand Junction 8
    Lancaster & Preston 8
    London & Birmingham 8
    Liverpool & Manchester 8
    Manchester & Birmingham 8
    North Union 8
    Wigan Branch 8
  British Standard 9
  LNWR standard 7, 9, 12-13
    axle load 12
    ballast 7, 12-13
    chairs 8, 10-11, 13
    fastenings 10-11
    fishplates 8-9, 11
    keys 8-9
  Rails
    iron 8-9
    steel 8-9
    steel-headed 9
  sleepers 10

Permanent Way Company, The 8

Personalities
  Allan, Alexander 42
  Bore, Richard 88
  Bury, Edward 43
  Cawkwell, William 43
  Cooke, C.J. Bowen 43
  Locke, Joseph 8
  McConnell, J.E. 42
  Moon, Richard 42
  Moorsom, Admiral 42
  Park, J.C. 94, 160
  Ramsbottom, John 42
  Slater 87-8
  Trevithick, A.F. 135
  Trevithick, Francis 42
  Vignoles, Charles 8
  Webb, Francis William 43
  Whale, George 43
  Worsdell, N 87-8

Platform trolleys 28, 31, 35

Poster boards 31, 146

R

Railways
    Bolton & Leigh 86
    Caledonian 135
    Chester & Holyhead 129
    Crewe & Chester 8
    East & West India Docks &
      Birmingham Junction 2
    Grand Junction 42, 86
    Lancashire & Yorkshire 2, 43, 58
    Leeds, Bradford & Halifax
      Junction 45
    Liverpool & Manchester 1, 42, 86, 129
    London & Birmingham 42-3, 86
    Manchester & Birmingham 42
    North Union 86, 143
    Preston & Wyre 2, 143
    Wigan Branch 8

Railway Clearing House 23

Railway Shareholders Manual 8

Refreshment trolleys 31, 35

Rugs 117

Rug and pillow trolley 31, 35

S

Saxby & Farmer 21-2

Sears Crossing 34

Shed plates 75-6

Shugborough Park 20

Shunting gong 23

Sidelamps, carriage stock 117, 163

Siemens & Martin steel 9

Signal boxes
    exterior finish 19, 24
    interior finish 24

Signals
    arms 20
    bi-directional 21
    bracket 20
    calling on 20
    distant 20
    gantry 20, 24
    ground 20, 24
      disc 20
      semaphore 20
    posts 20
    shunt 20
    slow and goods line 20
    spectacle glasses 22
    spectacles 20

Spring blinds 117

Sources
    Bennett, Rosling 47, 49
    Dickens, Charles 43
    Moore, F. 71
    Nelson, Jack 16
    Scott, S.S. 56
    Stretton, Charles E. 47
    Twining, E.W. 49

Station
    awnings 29
    buildings
      stone 26
      wood 26, 38
    canopies 29
    fences 13, 27
    nameboards 31
    screens 29
    seats 31, 35
    signs 31

Stations
    Aylesbury 30, 37
    Bedford (St Johns) 21
    Cheddington 40
    Claydon 36
    Crewe 8
    Cuddington (CLC) 31
    Glasson 30
    Gowerton 26-7
    Holly Bush 26-7
    Marsh Gibbon & Poundon 26, 29
    Oxford 26, 28
    Parsley Hay 35
    Ridgmont 26, 28
    Rugby 32
    Shap 26, 29
    Thrapston 24
    Verney Junction 28, 34

Steam Sheds 38-9
    Coleham 39
    Crewe South 39

T

Teak, Burma 92, 103, 162

U

Upholstery
- american cloth — 117
- greenwich lino — 117
- in first class — 117, 120
- in second class — 117, 121
- in third class — 117, 121
- leather — 121
- moquette — 121-2
- moroccan leather — 117
- rep — 117, 122
- velveteen — 122

V

Vans
- banana — 139
- brake — 123, 135-6
- butter — 129
- fish — 106
- goods — 129, 133
- gunpowder — 129
- milk — 106-7, 123
- motor car — 105, 111, 113
- newspaper — 108
- Palethorpes — 108, 114
- parcel — 123
- Pryce & Jones — 108, 114
- refrigerator — 129, 133, 143
- WCJS — 106, 143

Varnish — 61, 125-6

W

Wagons
- ballast — 139, 141
- bolster — 143
- cattle — 128, 136
- coal — 128, 131, 133
- glass — 135
- merchandise — 128
- open — 135
- service stock — 129
- tare weight on — 143
- timber — 143

Wagon sheets — 143

Water columns — 38

Water tanks — 38

'Webb' chair screw — 11-12

'Webb' hut — 28

Weight plates, carriages — 115

Woodwork, carriages
- Burma teak — 92, 103, 162
- mahogany — 123
- sycamore — 123
- walnut — 123

Works
- Crewe — 42, 87
- Earlestown — 128, 143
- Edge Hill — 42
- Longsight — 42
- Saltley — 87
- Willesden — 10
- Wolverton — 42, 87